SESSIONS WITH JUDGES

Smyth & Helwys Publishing, Inc.
6316 Peake Road
Macon, Georgia 31210-3960
1-800-747-3016
© 2017 by Charles Qualls

Library of Congress Cataloging-in-Publication Data

Names: Qualls, Charles, author.
Title: Sessions with Judges : colorful characters and powerful tales / by Charles
Qualls.
Description: Macon : Smyth & Helwys, 2017. | Includes bibliographical
references.
Identifiers: LCCN 2017019426 | ISBN 9781573129565 (pbk. : alk. paper)
Subjects: LCSH: Bible. Judges--Textbooks.
Classification: LCC BS1305.55 .Q35 2017 | DDC 223/.320071--dc23
LC record available at https://lccn.loc.gov/2017019426

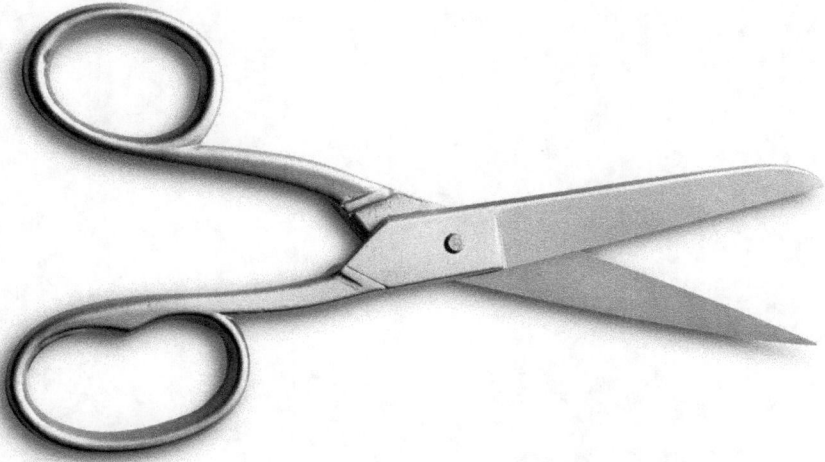

Sessions *with*
• • • Judges

Colorful Characters
and *Powerful Tales*

Charles Qualls

SMYTH&HELWYS
PUBLISHING, INCORPORATED   MACON, GEORGIA

*To those who have taught me more about the Bible,
especially the professors and pastors along the way.
And, to those who have studied with me.
Sunday school classes and groups have taught me
as we learned together.
There is still so much yet to discover.*

Contents

Introducing Judges ix

Session 1 1
A Promised Land Not Fully Claimed
Judges 1:1–2:5

Session 2 9
Which God Will You Serve?
Judges 2:6–3:6

Session 3 15
Ehud: Deception by a Lefty
Judges 3:7-30

Session 4 23
Deborah Lights a Fire and Jael Drives a Stake
Judges 4:1-24

Session 5 31
Gideon, Part 1: Don't Be Mad at Me, God
Judges 6:25-40

Session 6 39
Gideon, Part 2: Gideon's Army Is Too Large
Judges 7:1-25

Session 7 47
Abimelech: The Cost of Disloyalty and Greed
Judges 9:1-57

Session 8 53
Jephthah: Has God Had Enough?
Judges 10:6–11:28

Session 9 61
Samson: Strong and Smart for a Purpose
Judges 13:1-7; 16:4-31

Session 10 69
A Disturbing End
Judges 17–21

Bibliography 77

Introducing Judges

When I was sixteen years old, I was involved in a serious head-on automobile crash. Flown to the hospital due to my injuries, I soon recovered enough to enjoy the most intimidating experience of my life to that point: a date in court. Yes, the accident was my fault. The judge was someone I did not know in any way. Inside his courtroom, I found him to be one of the scariest humans I had ever encountered. He quickly took my plea and then set about deciding my punishment. A fine of some sort would be the minimum I could hope for. Quickly, though, he asked me how I would pay such a fine. I had no money at the time, and he growled something about it not being fair to expect my parents to pay for my negligence. Before I could blink, he announced that the fine would be suspended pending my completion of a defensive driving course. And, if that weren't terrifying enough—being found guilty and sentenced—he added a warning: "If you ever come in front of me again in a court, I will unseal your fine and add probation before we ever hear what else you've done!"

As an adult, I came to know that same judge as a fellow church member in my hometown. I would learn that he was the father of one of my high school classmates. In short, I was thankful for the opportunity to know him as a human being outside his job. Decades later, as a minister, I was asked to serve on a dedication program. The courthouse in downtown Atlanta was to be renamed in honor of one of my then-church members. On the day of the ceremony, I noticed that this same judge from my hometown was in the vast crowd. In front of dignitaries and the media, I brought a ripple of laughter as I stood at the podium. "Judge Hilliard," I said, "you once told me that if I ever appeared in front of you again at a courthouse you would unseal my suspended fine and add probation. Does this count?"

Judges are powerful people in the American culture. In almost any setting, their very title adds a sobering and focused tone. Most of us respect and fear them. We prefer that they protect us and maintain order. But, truthfully, we don't want much to do with them. Has this been your general experience?

As we start our sessions with Judges, let me ask you a question or two:

• When you hear that we are going to study from the book of Judges, what is your reaction?
• What is your understanding of the office or title of "judge" within ancient Hebrew life?
• Have you personally known anyone who was an actual judge? If so, what qualities of theirs come to mind?

My guess is that you picture a courtroom at the mere mention of the word "judges." Immediately, a sense comes over you that you should be careful. Perhaps the word "judge" makes you a little quieter. You have no doubt imagined a person seated behind a sizeable desk, elevated over everyone else in the room, ruling by law and by intimidation. This person has the power to jail you or at least to remove you from his or her presence. You arrive in the outfit you have chosen, likely a respectful and dressy one. The judge sits in a dark robe, utterly apart from anyone there by appearance.

Did any particularly positive or negative impressions come to mind as you considered actual judges you have watched or known? In either event, the qualities you imagined will come in handy, for you are about to study smart and proven individuals in the biblical book of Judges. But you are also about to encounter colorful characters whose excesses and flaws rise quickly to the surface.

Why Study Judges?

Advances in technology, industry, and knowledge over the last few thousand years might make the Old Testament era appear irrelevant. Several historic periods have intervened since the time of the Judges, yet one of the qualities that makes Scripture so timeless is that humanity itself changes very little. To be clear, the book of Judges covers essentially the time between when Israel was first occupying the promised land until later as Israel became hungry for a recognizable king.

A starting place as to why one might want to study from Judges is found in the word itself. *Shophetim* ("judges") was the Hebrew word for "deliverers" or "saviors." Other expressions for this role include "one who sets things straight" or "one who rules." The word *shophetim* occurs only twenty times in the book of Judges, and its participle (*shophet* or judge) only appears six times. Nowhere in this text is a single personality referred to directly as a *shophet*. Instead, a whole list of people—including those we will study more closely—is referred to as carrying out the functions of the *shophetim*.

There are both Greek and Latin words used in Scripture that more closely denote a judge or decider as we might more typically think in English. But those words do not bring the full context of the *shophetim* to their usages elsewhere in Scripture. Other extra-biblical sources (i.e., sources from outside the Bible) that depict this general period and locale also use the Hebrew concept of judges the way the book of Judges uses it. Scholar Jacob Myers notes that the Roman historian Livy is said to have compared these Hebrew judges with the later consuls of Rome (Myers, 677).

Depicted here in the book of Judges is the period in which a band of tribes, newly freed from Egypt, now occupies a foreign land. What may be hard for the reader to grasp is that Judges does not present the story of a comprehensive and united Israel. The wording in the book of Judges could suggest that a given leader ruled throughout the land. That is certainly the way I grew up understanding these stories. And, sometimes these characters may have indeed set a pace that influenced many tribes at once. But, at times their biblical stories also may have depicted only a regional or even local reality. There is no easy way to clear this up.

For our purposes, we will focus on the issues, personalities, actions, and results. We will worry less about a precise understanding of just how widespread the individual judge's power may have been. Clearly, their stories are important enough that they became a part of the collection of episodes we call Judges. Until the time of the kings, there simply was no completely unified Israel—though our Bible will often voice these stories as though there were.

Moses and Joshua mostly presided over a unified people. They delivered the children of Israel through the generations, ultimately reaching and settling in Canaan. But, as we pick up these stories, the tribes have now reached their space allotments. They have set up a way of life that was fairly independent of one another. When the kings do come about later, we will see once again a unified Israel for a time. But, not so in this biblical book.

Formally descending "kings" had not yet become a glimmer in the Israelites' eyes. Still, these humans were clearly not capable of following God's greatest hopes without some guidance. Under Moses and Joshua, there appears to have been some semblance of cooperation and progress. Similar leaders would be needed, and they are enumerated here in this book. They are not as readily identified as being chosen directly by God as were Moses or Joshua. However, we will see God closely involved with many of them as they lead.

We should be fascinated to observe that there was a rather mystical quality to these Hebrew judges. Several of them, perhaps most obviously Samson, are portrayed as having almost mythical abilities or characteristic bestowed on them directly by God. For some, this is most noticeable in their wisdom. For others, physical strength or other pronounced abilities are evident. Still others appear to have been the most savvy and strategic of leaders when faced with opportunities for conquest and when dealing with surrounding threats. There is no clear understanding from the text as to how these leaders assumed the status of *shophetim*. We are forced, in some measure, to take these stories as they are—gaps and all.

If we still want to exercise our traditional understandings of a judge, then Myers notes that only Deborah and Samuel are depicted as rendering decisions in actual cases. The others likely did so as well. These characters led in multiple realms that may have ranged from military to civil and beyond. No doubt God's leadership was upon them as they brought a sense of order to groups that badly needed it.

Why should we be interested in the study of Judges? There are several reasons:

• This transitional period in Israel's history mirrors our current age spiritually. We live in a time in which we find ourselves wandering as a faith group. Certainly, Christianity today is being challenged from without and within. Once a powerful majority in America, believers are now finding that their faith is viewed in a more skeptical and devalued light. Who and what will guide Christians today?

• The Judges "cycle" (we will revisit this idea later as a theme) should be instructive for our own living. That is, their periods of wandering and need, reflection and repentance, penalty and restoration reflect our own spiritual realities. Judges should be both a cautionary and an encouraging book.

• For many of us, freedom and boundless options are realities of life. In our abundance, much should be expected of us. Sometimes we make constructive or healthy choices. Other times we let down both our God and our peers. We need guidance to help us make the best choices each day. The lessons of Judges speak to some of the freedom we enjoy as well as the decision making we must do.

• These stories really are our stories! Despite the accelerated abilities or accomplishments of the characters in Judges, we should be slow to place them on pedestals. In other words, their stories need to remain our stories. There is danger in elevating any biblical figure (aside from Christ himself) to the realm of hero. When we do, we have precious little to learn from them because their stories become something to watch and cheer for rather than something to relate to and learn from.

• We learn much about God in the narratives, specifically from the interactions attributed to God with the judges and other characters. As the better qualities of the various judges shine, we see the greatest hopes and priorities of God. What they have been given by God will often reflect qualities found in each of us, at least in some measure. How will we use those same gifts? What they do wisely, or well, will often reflect something that God hopes to achieve in humanity throughout history. How will we each contribute toward God's efforts in those ways?

Still not persuaded of the value of studying Judges? After all, the above points sound rather academic and formal. Let's toss into the discussion some of the more intriguing reasons to study Judges. J. Clinton McCann (1–2), adds these reasons the church should not miss out on this segment of holy Scripture.

First, does tension between rival groups in the Middle East sound familiar? That is exactly what is portrayed in Judges, complete with disputes over land or territorial rights. Second, there is uncertainty over the roles of men and women in leadership. Our American political scene continues to address gender evolution even as I write. You'll see that theme boldly portrayed in Judges. Next, power-hungry political leaders are on display in these pages. Most readers can't seem to get enough of such headlines! Speaking of headlines, child abuse, spousal abuse, and senseless or excessive violence are found in the chapters of Judges. We also see powerful political leaders who are distracted by sexual temptation. Tellingly, themes of excessive individualism, moral confusion, and social chaos occupy the pages of this book. Does God have your attention with this Scripture now?

God's ways are life-giving. They are no more restrictive than we need. If we live within God's intent, then life is generally orderly and safe. That is, at least as much as we can choose for ourselves. Others must also choose whether to live within or without God's hopes for humanity. God would grant health, well-being, and peace—*shalom*—but this will always be up to people to embrace or reject.

Who Wrote the Book of Judges?

If there were one question I would hope to dodge about Judges, this would be the one. *Who wrote the book of Judges?* And you, the reader, would be well within your rights to ask that. Questions about why the book is so violent, how these stories reconcile with a loving God, and even what connections we can make to our own lives seem easy by comparison. But who wrote Judges?

In short, no one person seems to have written this Old Testament book. Instead, it is a compilation from several different sources. From oral tradition to narrative, this book collects some of the best information available from Hebrew antiquity to depict a wild era of settlement.

Jacob Myers, for one, believes that the original form of Judges did not begin with the current 1:1. In fact, he holds that 1:1–2:5 and 17:1–21:25 were probably added by the final editor (Myers, 680). A section from 2:6–16:31 is known as the "Deuteronomic" edition of the book of Judges. Scholars say that since 2:6-9 essentially repeats the history from the previous book of Joshua (see Josh 24:28-31), the book of Judges likely once began with those verses; therefore, the bulk of the work is sometimes referred to as having been recorded by "the Deuteronomist" or the "Deuteronomic editor."

Myers posits that the second or final editors of Judges might have come from the regions of Dan or Benjamin, based on their knowledge of and sympathy with these peoples. Similarities in style and agenda to the Pentateuch of the Old Testament suggest that the material in chapters 17–21 was especially drawn from a similar (if not the same) source. A fascinating note is that Judges 1:10-15, 20 echoes Joshua 15:13-19. Other close parallels can be drawn from parts of Judges 1 and entries found in Joshua 15–17. They appear to have been drawn from very much the same source.

All of this leads to one observation. The exploration of the multiple sources from which this book springs may be a little dizzying to follow, but the speculation and parallels prove quite fascinating. Some parts remind one of the L source, while others sound like JE and J sources of Scripture texts (Myers, 678).

Let's take a quick look at the ancient sources of manuscripts from which our collected or canonized Bible emerged. For instance, the "L" source (for *Laienquelle* and sometimes referred to as a subset of the J, or specifically, the J2 source) is regarded to be the oldest of the biblical sources. The editor who compiled these stories in Judges probably had some agenda or obligation beyond mere storytelling, just as any publisher does. He chose to draw from multiple sources, as either fit the need or were simply what was available. So, while L might have been the older source, it was neither the only source nor the most complete source. Other material came from the J1 source. Whereas the "J" sources used "Yahweh" or "Jahweh" as the Hebrew name for God, the "E" source writings used "Elohim" as a proper name for God. The E source is more often associated as coming from a Northern kingdom sympathy. The J-sourced biblical writings related more closely to Southern kingdom roots. To further complicate, a later editor or redactor combined the J and E sources, giving us the JE source that some will refer to.

When Was Judges Written and What Period Does It Cover?

How old is the book of Judges? We might imagine some Indiana Jones figure finding the ancient scroll and somehow testing the text to determine its age. We might wish for a historical record that documents the writing of Judges.

Our problem is that fixing a close time of composition for this text is simply too difficult. Speculating on who pulled together the material that we recognize as Judges and roughly when it was collected is an evolved effort. As with so many biblical texts, one needs to recognize the work of God and a few individuals who collectively "authored" the writings over a stretch of time. A few drafts appear to have been made.

The work of pulling together the stories in Judges probably took place over hundreds of years after the actual period when these leaders lived and served. Particularly tricky is estimating just how long—and to what extent—these local heroes' exploits were repeated orally and passed along before being written down. It is also difficult to establish that any one of these judges ever ruled over "all" of Israel. Unfortunately, the collected and unified people we know as Israel simply does not seem to match the era of these stories, even if they are represented as such within the book of Judges.

McCann helps us greatly here with a term of Latin derivation: "liminal" (7). This word suggests a place of "threshold, margin or border." This is an apt physical and metaphoric description. In the time of Judges, the people called "Israel" lived in some newly granted borders and margins of land already occupied by Canaan. They were trying to come in and take over what had been "promised" to them. But things were by no means settled. The people of Israel will appear in these texts as obviously marginal. What is the metaphor, then? If one glances backward at their era of Egyptian slavery, and later at their defined kingdoms, Israel was very much a liminal people in the time of the judges. Very little was settled, whether in location or leadership. Their relationship with God was still being fleshed out, at least regarding their organized or collected participation as a faith group. They were living in, around, and in-between. I have a Jewish friend who will sometimes describe something as being caught in "liminal time" because she is so in touch with that part of her heritage. They had arrived in a place, their promised place, but because of the region's complexities, learning how to live there would take generations.

Committing to an *era* that this material depicts is a somewhat easier task. Many scholars believe the writing covers 1200–1020 BC (Myers, 680–86). That much can be deduced from biblical and extra-biblical sources. The exodus from Egypt seems to have taken place around 1280 BC. The conquest of the land fell somewhere between 1250 and 1200. Having arrived, the groups of Israelites seem to have formed what is referred to as a tribal league. It appears that the judges were in charge of this league or rose to be the focal heads that these league members responded to best. There were so-called "major" judges (Othniel, Ehud, Deborah, Gideon, Jephthah, Samson) and "minor" ones (Shamgar, Tola, Jair, Ibzan, Elon, Abdon). This difference is mostly based on the material available in the book. There are either twelve or thirteen judges in all (depending on whether Abimelech is counted).

Why Was Judges Written?

The late Joseph Callaway said that one of the most vexing problems for biblical archaeologists might be substantiating and documenting the period many refer to as the "conquest of Canaan." Some of his hands-on exploration took place in the areas of ancient Jericho (Tell es-Sultan) and a place called "Ai," just a few miles north of Jerusalem and about a mile east of a biblical site named Bethel. Callaway was regarded during his teaching career as one of the eminent scholars on Israel's emergence in Canaan.

This Baptist scholar reminds us that there is a long way to go before archaeology will be able to shed helpful light on so many of the questions, curiosities, and stories of our Bible. One can get the impression that the conquest of Israel was something that happened in a relatively short time. This is simply not so. But, scholars struggle to find ways to clarify a more exact time span. And the problems are not only archaeological.

For instance, the book of Judges takes some issue with the book of Numbers (chapter 10), wherein we are told that under Joshua the land of Canaan was taken decisively and completely in a five-year period. In contrast, Judges opens by saying that at the death of Joshua, the Israelites had not yet taken any of the land of Canaan. A unified Israel is not necessarily depicted in Judges, either. Instead, battles by various tribes or groups within the larger whole seem much more common.

We will hear a list of about twenty cities that the Israelite factions were not able to take over successfully. Among these are Megiddo, Gezer, and Jerusalem in Judges 1:21-29 (see Callaway, 85–87). Callaway goes on to cite other instances where the accounts of Joshua and Numbers differ from that of Judges. And there are even some instances where there are discrepancies within Joshua. For example, chapters 10 and 11 make dramatic and final claims about his marvelous victories. But then in chapter 13 the same book lists areas still to be taken that include some previously listed as safely in the hands of Israel. Joshua 10 talks about the complete conquest of the "hill" country, including Hebron and Debir, as led by Joshua. Then, in the fifteenth chapter of that book, credit for those battles is given to Caleb (Hebron) and Othniel (Debir) (Callaway, 88).

We will not solve these problems within this study. These grand stories raise many other types of questions for us as well. But they also paint a human picture that should prove instructive to biblical readers, for their patterns can easily be seen in our own behaviors. Their approaches to God will resemble our spiritual tendencies. In our most contrite moments, their desperation will sound like our desperation. They will pledge allegiance and purpose to God just like you and I often do. They will bargain, plead, and cajole.

The Greek-inspired term *amphyctyony* denotes a "religious confederacy united around ownership at a central sanctuary." This alignment might also be described as "a league of tribes formed around a common religious commitment" (Flanders et al., 202–203). As far back as the tribes leaving Egypt with Moses and entering Canaan under Joshua's leadership, they fulfilled the covenant promise they had entered into around the area of Shechem. There they reestablished relationships with kindred tribes already inhabiting the area. And Hebrew elements in the south (portions of Judah and kindred tribes) also joined the group that had entered under Joshua.

All of this suggests that by the time of the Judges, the picture that many of us have grown up with (a united if fledgling Israel) might not be the most helpful one for understanding our holy Scripture. The book of Judges, then, lays open this fractured and unstable alliance.

Have you noticed that preachers don't often bring sermons from Judges to the pulpit? In Bible studies, your group leader probably won't often say, "I have found the most uplifting passages in Judges, and we are going to study them today!" Even less likely would be your children coming home from Vacation Bible School having studied from portions of Judges, aside from the wonderful stories about Samson and Delilah. This book, however, offers significant lessons for believers.

The Judges' Cycle and Key Themes

One should consider a binding formula widely recognized as "The Judges' Cycle." My own summary of this cyclical pattern includes these elements: *apostasy, oppression, repentance,* and *deliverance.* The reader of these stories will notice that this pattern seems basic to almost all of Judges. A similar pattern is found in the later Old Testament books of the Prophets. We do well to set straight this reality: God did not direct or guide these elements to happen to the people. Rather, these movements unfolded because of human nature. When these stories become our stories, we cannot help recognizing our own proclivity to similar patterns of behavior. Most of us experience times in our lives where we are closer to or more distant from God. We are sometimes more and sometimes less open to God's desires. We are faithful and loyal in our best of times, and we are sinful and broken in our worst.

These are the tales of real people. They serve a great purpose beyond entertainment, though some portions of them are very entertaining. The intent of these stories is to preserve the truths of an era in history. Perhaps they do that far better than preserving actual historic facts. These truths, such as the judges' cycle, instruct us. They teach us about God and about ourselves.

Additionally, there are key themes to note in this book. Knowing them ahead of time will keep the devotional student, and the group discussion, a bit more focused. When taken only as a collection of dramatic stories—and sometimes repulsively violent ones—this material will occasionally distract the reader. We can get closer to the biblical intent, I believe, when we are mindful of these themes:

• Human frailty apart from God
• God's watchful state over creation
• God's responsiveness to a sincere and repentant humanity
• The assessment of life through theological filters
• The covenants of God that stay in place across generations—and millennia—of human history
• A warning that disloyalty and disobedience leads to consequences
• God's offer of help and hope if humanity will accept it

Join me as we walk through this important book of Scripture together.

A Promised Land
Not Fully Claimed

Begin by reading Judges 1:1-10.
We notice that these opening passages operate matter-of-factly. They report a fast-moving sequence of action with little detail. Still, their contents are quite important. So, while this first session provides an overview to the early battles of the Judges' period, other themes and observations need to be stated. We will take the opportunity in this less-narrative opening to explore some elements that flavor the book of Judges.

Unfinished Business

Judges opens with a deep contrast to the information found in the book of Joshua. Joshua's material would lead one to believe that in a series of skirmishes, played out over five years or so, the Israelites took Canaan for themselves and occupied their promised land.

In contrast, Judges shows that as Joshua died, the Hebrews were perhaps a few generations away from taking the land. Many bloody battles lay ahead. In the introduction, we noted that there were some twenty key cities still to take, including Jerusalem, which may be the most noteworthy of the group.

Immediately, we begin to wonder, *who were the Canaanites?* If you grew up like me, you understood this to be one unified people. The reality here in Judges is that "Canaanites" is a more general term used to refer to any previous inhabitants of Palestine.

In verse 1, the issue about taking the promised territory is stated. *Who shall go up?* Jacob Myers believes that this question as recorded in Judges 1 was both asked and answered by the Lord as they put the question to the "lot" system. This was what the Israelites referred to as "the oracle of the Lord." They might have reached into a jar and drawn out pre-inscribed stones in a case like this. The system was used throughout the ancient world, with some variations. In this instance, it seems Judah was the lot drawn.

We do well to remember the basic framework or "cycle" of the Judges:

• The people of God sin; they do some type of "evil" in God's eyes. (2:11-13; 3:7, 12; 4:1; 6:1; 10:6; 13:1)
• God is upset with them, angry at their lack of loyalty and discipline. God permits their enemies to occupy, overtake, or exile them. (2:14-15; 3:8, 12-14; 4:2; 6:1-5; 10:7-10; 13:1)
• God raises up a judge or a savior, a deliverer, after hearing the cries of the people. (2:18; 3:9, 15; 4:3-10; 6:6-18; 10:10-16)
• The judge dies, and the people embark on a new time of wayward drift. Idolatry is often a chief offense. Disobedience evolves. (2:19)

It is important to keep this "cycle" perspective in mind as we read Judges. If we don't, then this becomes just a collection of stories.

These judges rose to prominence in a variety of ways. A common factor, though, is the people's relative nearness to God that seems to arrive in conjunction with each leader's rise. As long as the leader was in place, the relationship between God and people appeared to work acceptably. But when a given judge left the scene, things appeared to go bad.

In the larger picture, we should notice that the judges appear to become increasingly less effective in their roles as the book of Judges progresses. We will see some of that in these sessions.

In summary, the chief indictment in the book of Judges is that the people went into the territory and did not carry out the commands of God regarding how to set up the promised land. (We will look at the particulars in Judges 2:1-5 later.)

Flavors, Tones, and Biases

As an aside, these early pages in Judges 1 begin to illuminate some interesting features of the book.

Some scholars find the book of Judges to be sympathetic with the people of Judah. While at this time there was technically one unified kingdom, later ancient Hebrew history will acknowledge a divided kingdom: Israel (the north) and Judah (the south). Judges 1:1–2:5 is widely assumed to be a later add-on to the larger Deuteronomical section of Judges. McCann is specific in theorizing that this section may have been added during the time when King David's leadership was being compared with that of Saul. Judah was very much a part of David's throne.

In contrast, the tribe of Benjamin does not far well, and neither does Gibeah, an important town in the tribe's territory. Both Benjamin and Gibeah were associated more closely with King Saul's court, and this observation partially makes McCann's case. Their shortcomings and weaknesses will be pulled to the front in Judges. One could believe that this slant points toward some propaganda usage of Judges during David's time. This suspicion comes more from the slant that various scholars detect more so than any specific historic evidence of having seen this regional propaganda in use. But, there does seem at times to be a favor of Judah, particularly in the first and last chapters of Judges.

Theology

We should watch for some theological lessons. Among them are the following:

1. The people of God have responsibilities. First among them might be to assemble and worship God actively and together. They also have specific duties for the decisive occupation of the promised land. Judges 1:1-10 demonstrates this vividly.

2. God's sovereignty is in place. In Judges 1, God is ready to direct the chosen people to their land. God worked among the people and chose to help them in their faithfulness. Likewise, God will be depicted later as pulling away from them in their less faithful periods—in a very specific way—leaving them largely to the consequences of their deeds and their distance. Gideon is an example of a leader who will affirm later that God is their sovereign head.

3. An Old Testament view of sin shines through here: the "cause-effect" understanding of God's action in people's lives. When things go well for the people, they chalk it up to their faithfulness and obedience to God. Notice how Judges 1:1-10 shows the early battles going well for the Hebrews. Conversely, when things go bad later, it is seen as a response to the people's sin. We will revisit this theme many times in our sessions.

4. The Judges' Cycle says something about the greatest power God has—love. God stubbornly and patiently and repeatedly responds and brings Israel back from the desolation of their collective souls.

5. McCann also believes that the book of Judges does something else: it takes on a prophetic quality in its content. The people of God throughout time are cautioned about the hurtful results of disobedience. And we are issued here a repeated call to draw nearer and be faithful!

Read Judges 1:11-21.
The battles continue in this section. Notice the brazen offer that Caleb makes to spur on the spirit of conquest. In verse 12, "He who attacks Kiriathsepher and takes it, I will give Achsah my daughter as wife." Othniel, who was either his young nephew or brother (either translation seems possible), took up the challenge and won the battle. Thus, he also won the hand of Achsah, Caleb's daughter, and a prized segment of land.

There is much here to which we may not relate so readily. An immediate relative just won the hand of his niece or cousin by winning a battle? Paul wrote in Romans 15:4, "For whatsoever things were written aforetime were written for our learning" (KJV). But what can we learn from a text like this?

As hard as it may be for us to understand the instructions to drive out and destroy (that is, kill) the inhabitants of a desired land, this is the report we find in Judges. We will see later the consequences of not obeying God. This people of God, who were intended to live as an alternative culture under God's direction, instead became intermingled with the Canaanite factions that they allowed to remain.

We will see the people of Israel begin to dabble in other religions and traditions. They would use a piece of this faith and a bit of that practice—all open-mindedly and making good sense to them at the time. Does any of this sound familiar to us today?

One caution to the reader here: we need to take great care in our study. This book was crafted and structured with the theological outlook of the era in which it was written. Secondary (or "human") causation had not yet occurred to them as a people. That is, everything, good or bad, was assumed to be a sign of God's blessing and favor or of God's annoyance and displeasure. We should try as much as possible to study these texts in that light. Though some of the instructions—and interpretations that Judges will give—are perplexing, the reigning theology of the day will be our most useful filter.

The choice to let some of the people stay in these territories is a curious matter. On the one hand, we will see it characterized as an unfaithful choice by God's people. On the other, we will see notes like that of Judges 1:16-21. In verse 19, God's people seem unable to flush out the inhabitants of the valley even though God has delivered the mountain country completely into their hands. These valley-dwellers are seen to have "chariots of iron." Apparently, their might and their formidable equipment make them resistant to leaving the area. In verse 20, God's people are successful in taking Hebron but not in driving out the Jebusites who inhabited Jerusalem and who are seen to dwell with Benjamin "unto this day." As we noted earlier, some editorials embedded in this opening session of Judges favor Judah but not Benjamin. Benjamin is depicted here as either being weak or unfaithful to God's instructions.

Read Judges 1:22–2:5.
As we expect, the battles continue in this section. By now, following the action is becoming a daunting task for the reader. In this section, we read a list of villages where the inhabitants were not driven out. Yet the people of Israel had been told to do exactly that. We notice the setting up of cohabitations between the new settlers and the previous inhabitants.

How do you react to this in your heart? Many of us might observe that this arrangement seems more humane. If God has sent the Hebrews to conquer an already occupied land, then finding a way live with the defeated inhabitants sounds "Christian" to our modern ears.

Here is where obedience to God becomes a conflicting issue. If God commanded them to drive out the previous inhabitants, then which value should prevail? Why would God have told them to clear the land of its previous people?

In the long run, we know that intermingling with the inhabitants caused less than satisfactory results. The people would give their hearts to God, but not completely. They would worship God, but not completely. They would live according to the Law, but not completely. A lingering theme is that their mixing with the native remnants kept them distracted from becoming the holy nation that God intended.

How do you evaluate this situation from your reading of the larger biblical text?

Now, in the opening verses of chapter 2, we hear the judgment of God. Specifically, in verses 1-5 there is a sad unfolding of God's disappointment and the people's remorse. "But you have not obeyed my command," God says. "What is this you have done?" We can see how strongly God felt about a people's remaining faithful to creation's greatest hopes. This was requisite in the eyes of God, yet hard for humanity to live up to.

But the turning point that sets a strong flavor for the rest of the book is waiting in verse 3: "So now, I say, I will not drive them out before you; but they shall become adversaries to you, and their gods shall be a snare to you."

What do you hear God pronouncing upon them? And, based on your knowledge of the larger biblical canon, what do you believe this will come to mean for Israel?

This is a harsh judgment from God. We can hear the foreshadowing of approaching hardship. A case is made here for why Israel will suffer in later times. If one is seeking to understand the background for much of the Old Testament's ebb and flow, this section of Judges is key.

Remember that from a literary standpoint, the biblical niche that Judges occupies is to tell the story of Israel from the time of the deaths of Moses and Joshua until the time covered in 1 and 2 Samuel. At that point, the kings will arrive to take their turn guiding the people. They too will be charged with keeping the people in a close relationship with God. Like the judges, these later kings will discover that that the peoples' early disobedience set up a difficult mixture of cultures in which they live. Generations struggled with faithfulness to God's ways while trying to live in a polytheistic reality. These people groups influenced each other, and the Israelites constantly dabbled in forms of worship dedicated to other gods. How does this shed light for you on modern Israel and the Palestinian struggles? What of today's issues seem merely to be a continuation of biblical Israel's tribal strife? What elements make this different today?

1. When you think of the biblical "judges," how would you describe the role these people were to play? How do they differ from judges today?

_____

_____

_____

_____

_____

2. In Israel's leadership, where did the judges fit between strong personalities such as Abraham, Moses, or Joshua versus the kings who would come later?

_____

_____

_____

_____

_____

3. How do you understand God's intent that the Hebrew nation should take over the land of Canaan completely, even driving out all the previous inhabitants?

_____

_____

_____

_____

_____

4. How do you put the violence found in the Old Testament within your perspective of faith?

_____

_____

_____

_____

_____

5. What was the danger of God's people failing at or disobeying God's command to drive out the native inhabitants?

_____

_____

_____

_____

_____

A Promised Land Not Fully Claimed

6. In this study, we discussed the "Judges' Cycle." How does this help you understand a pattern between God and Israel during these days?

_____

_____

_____

_____

_____

7. Does the cycle relate to your life in any helpful way? In what ways do you find parallels to your life where you draw closer to—and further from—God?

_____

_____

_____

_____

_____

8. God chooses to leave Israel to its own consequences over the course of Judges. How do you react to God's choice? What does it have to do with how God relates to you?

_____

_____

_____

_____

_____

Which God Will You Serve?

Judges 2:6–3:6

Read Judges 2:6-15.

From the previous session, you may recall that some people consider the opening verses of Judges 2 to be a second introduction to the book. Judges 2:6 seems to fit particularly well with the end of the biblical book of Joshua, so there may in fact be a strong case that they were made to join in some sense (McCann, 34–35).

Professor Dan Kent observes that in our English Bibles, the book of Judges is the second book of the Deuteronomic History, a collection of writings from Joshua through 2 Kings that covers Israel's history from a Deuteronomic, or prophetic, perspective. These books show God's working among creation in general and through Israel in particular to bring about an intended purpose. To accomplish that purpose, God charged Israel with a specific set of duties.

Like a prophecy, the book of Judges brings an evaluation in addition to the storytelling. Part of Israel's burden of such a great responsibility was hearing their collective ledger read, detailing their faithfulness or their disloyalty. Kent feels that Judges establishes that

• God "is active in history and is carrying out purposes in history;
• history is the stage where God rewards the faithful and judges the disobedient, both nations and individuals;
• therefore, if Israel sinned, she was sure to be punished;
• and that deliverance would come only if she repented." (84)

Joshua 24:1-28 describes a covenant renewal ceremony of sorts. Kent refers to this as a "Continental Congress for Israel." In other words, as Joshua's time wound down, the reality was that Israel was a loosely organized confederation of tribes. There was no strong, central government. Before the kings rise to power, then, we will watch as a league of tribes searches for unity. Although the names of the individual tribes appear to have been certain, how they related to one another as the whole people "Israel" was much more inconsistent than many of us allow in our readings.

They did share a language, customs, history, and background. They could muster up some shared efforts at defense when needed. It appears there were times of worship together, and they held in common an ethical code and moral law. As Kent says, though, the binding force seems to have been more religious than social or political.

Judges 2:11 levels an accusation at the people. They did "what was evil in the sight of the LORD." The result was distance from their God who had delivered them from slavery in Egypt and who had brought them to this promised place. God was angry, so invaders had their way with some of the Hebrew people. They lost belongings and their relatively newfound status. This set the stage for the establishment of judges as decision-making leaders.

How do you feel about this unsteady relationship with God, from both the viewpoint of the people and the Almighty?

Read Judges 2:16-23.
Make no mistake: God was the leader and guide for the nation. The Lord was the King of Israel. The covenant affirmations from earlier reminded Israel that they were bound by Jehovah. Shiloh held the ark of the covenant and the tabernacle. There were also worship sites at Shechem, Bethel, and Gilgal. Shechem and Shiloh were the most powerful of the locations in which the people could gather and expect to be in God's presence. But, as human beings, they looked for a leader among them whom they could hear and see. They desired someone to follow and watch. After all, nations around them had monarchies.

At least one observer has called the period of the Judges "the Dark Ages of Hebrew history." It was a bloody period. Chaos seemed to rule as much as any human did. There was fighting, idolatry, and distracted living. We will watch the people of this book be violent, conniving, disloyal, and greedy. In fairness, we will also watch them display bravery, faithfulness, and the ability to do the right thing.

In chapter 2, starting with verse 11, we hear a specific accusation: the people are worshiping Ba'al. The Hebrew word "Ba'al" means *lord* or *master*.

The larger suggestion for Israel as a loose league of tribes might be that Ba'al symbolized their loyalty to various local gods and their adoption of local forms of worship. We tend to read about the occupation of Canaan and assume more than was actually happening. Here are some common misreadings:

• That all the people known as Israel spread out across the promised land and acted very much alike. We assume this because we believe that the Law and the wilderness wanderings had built them into a cohesive group. The reality is that they almost immediately began to intermingle with the remnants of previous peoples in their lands. A blending of cultures created a vast and diverse fusion.

• That wherever they may have been in these territories, they were living a similar lifestyle, eating the same foods, worshiping in similar ways, and understanding God with a unified ear. If we allow ourselves to consider this, we can understand how unlikely this unity of lifestyle could be. But we have romanticized the stories and ignored the clues given to us in books like Judges.

• That the one God, Yahweh, was the focus of Israel's unified heart. In reality, Judges tells us that local gods got fair play when Israel's people intermingled and began to open their hearts to what seemed accessible and more immediate. We may need to interpret Ba'al more broadly, for there were likely several local gods, all of whom could be understood as either a Ba'al (a male god figure) or as an Ashtaroth (a female counterpart to Ba'al).

So we have already made the important case that the *people* of Israel were actually many peoples. Earlier, we acknowledged that there would appear and reappear a pattern of interaction between God and Israel known as the "Judges' Cycle." In session 1, we learned how this cycle went. Thus the cycle—as described for us in Judges 2 across several paragraphs—will be presented as both a broader indictment of the people and a testimony to a more loving, patient, and gracious God than many are prepared to notice in an Old Testament setting.

The punishment of the disobedient people was often severe. That much is painfully clear. But the punishment is also an interesting thing to behold. Understandably, God's anger is represented in Judges. In our New Testament Christian hearts, we would probably offer synonyms that expand the understanding to include God's disappointment, heartbreak, and sorrow over the people's conduct.

J. Clinton McCann says that we must process the concept of *justice* as we read Judges. In this portion of the book of Judges, we may read justice as retribution—as God rewarding good people and punishing bad people. But McCann suggests that the language reveals something else. Namely, the same word is used to represent both the *evil* the Hebrews did and the *misfortune* they suffered. McCann says this allows for the possibility that what appears to be divine punishment is really the consequences or natural judgment of the people's own deeds (35–37).

First Samuel 8:1-18 portrays a larger issue of justice, finally resulting in a statement that the destructive effects of *the people's selfish choices* were caused by the king "whom you have chosen for yourselves" (v. 18). That is to say, they reaped what they sowed.

Some people cycle through employment problems for the length of their careers. A church member told me sometime back, "I am retired now, but I was fired from every job I ever had." If we witness that happening, we may eventually realize that no one person could likely be so unfortunate without having a hand in his or her own demise. As a friend once observed of a fellow minister in another state, "He's a great guy, but he can't stay out of his own way long enough to keep a church." Often, the difficulties people face are less the punishment of an angry God and more the natural consequences of their actions that God allows them to suffer.

Read Judges 3:1-6.

In this passage, the fracture in the relationship with God is illustrated to an extreme. The text says that God "left," or allowed to remain, rival nations in order to test Israel in battle. They were the Philistines, the Canaanites, the Sidonians, and the Hivites.

The text intimates that God left these groups to see whether the people would follow the commands of Yahweh as brought to them by Moses. The result appears to be a melding of people. The Israelites took the daughters of these peoples for their wives, and they took the gods of these peoples instead of the one true God they knew.

In these early scenes from Judges, we have studied a significant amount of background and detail. Study participants may long for the action to begin. For instance, we have not yet seen a judge assume leadership. However, if we have been faithful in studying through the first chapters, then our encounters with the characters will be of more benefit.

1. Review the events of the Judges' Cycle. What were the repeated actions of both God and the people?

_____

_____

_____

_____

_____

2. God was working through Israel for a specific purpose or set of purposes. How would you describe that sense of purpose for Israel?

_____

_____

_____

_____

_____

3. God's strict instruction about worship included a provision that Yahweh would be the only God receiving the people's allegiance. What makes God's "jealousy" understandable to the extent that Israel was later punished regarding this issue?

_____

_____

_____

_____

_____

4. If Ba'al was not a specific god, then what seems to be the understanding of this word? What were God's people worshiping?

_____

_____

_____

_____

_____

5. How would you define the concept of *justice*? Discuss this as a group.

_____

_____

_____

_____

_____

6. Why was justice already such a central concept to what God desired for Israel?

_____

_____

_____

_____

_____

7. How would you describe God's approach to *punishment* when humanity is unfaithful and distant?

_____

_____

_____

_____

_____

8. What strikes you as just about this punishment? Is there anything that seems unjust or difficult to comprehend?

_____

_____

_____

_____

_____

Ehud: Deception by a Lefty

In Baseball as in Life?

Did you know that some of the greatest pitchers in Major League baseball history have been left-handers? Lefty Grove was one of the more famous, with his nickname an obvious homage to his dominant hand. Warren Spahn won 363 games throwing as a "southpaw." As an Atlanta Braves fan, I would be remiss not to name one of our lefty greats—Tom Glavine. Mickey Mantle's famous sidekick, Whitey Ford, was left-handed. And a lefty pitcher by the name of Babe Ruth won ninety-four games before Red Sox team owners decided he was too valuable as a hitter not to have in the lineup every day. So they kept him in right field, and he did pretty well at the plate!

Why is being left-handed so important in baseball? Some feel that a left-hander in baseball has distinct advantages as a pitcher and as a hitter. A statistical reality is that more pitchers are right-handed and more hitters are right-handed. The occasional left-hander is coveted for a pitching rotation because he or she offers an unusual delivery to hitters. More deception is possible for left-handers because batters have less opportunity to get used to the left-handed pitching style. Likewise, a hitter has more of an advantage visually when he or she bats from the opposite side of the plate as the pitcher's delivery. Since there are more right-handed pitchers, a lefty batter is a good commodity in a lineup. Stan Musial, Babe Ruth, Ken Griffey, Jr., and Ted Williams were all left-handed hitters.

Our first story in Judges features a lefty. Are any of you left-handed? If so, how has life been different for you than for right-handed people?

Read Judges 3:7-14.

Some details in this text seem odd. Some might even be a little gross. They stand out to us and raise questions. We will look at some of these as we go; just know that this may be a bit awkward. We are adults, though, and I trust that you can handle these curiosities. I promise not to raise these odd details merely for a giggle but to pull forward the powerful theology that they can share with us.

Here we recall the Judges' Cycle. That circle of life begins in faithfulness but eventually finds a people living apart from God. Life's inevitable hardships and punishment sent them reaching out to God for help. These judges would often lead them back to faithfulness, or intervene somehow with God. They were delivered from their hardship, and returned to a peace through their faithfulness. Remember the perpetual Judges' Cycle of sin, punishment, crying out for help, God's deliverance through a judge, and then Sabbath rest in the land? We will see that cycle in action in chapter 3.

As a bit of background to our focal story, we learn that Israel did evil, forgot the Lord, and worshiped other gods (the first step in the Judges' Cycle). God gave them over to a leader named King Cushan-rishathaim (step 2 in the cycle). The people cried out, and God gave them the first mentioned judge, Othniel, who led a renewed Israel in battle and delivered them (step 3). A period of some forty years was said to be peaceful, and then Othniel died (step 4).

After the death of Othniel, Israel swung into that predictable state of wandering. Again, they did evil in the Lord's sight, and the cycle started over. In an alliance with the "children of Ammon and Amalek," King Eglon of Moab rose up and "smote" Israel (3:13 KJV). The resulting eighteen years were a time of servilitude to Eglon and is the context of our session. The nation of Moab specifically invaded Israel in an area west of the Jordan River as far as the "city of palms." This ancient city, not identified on our maps, would seem to be Jericho. Eglon may even have reached as far as Bethel to wreak one of the two destructions, according to Jacob Myers in the *Interpreter's Bible Commentary* (708–709). Moab now controlled Israel as a territory.

Squandering Freedoms and Resources

In the 2000s, HBO network's popular series *The Sopranos* portrayed a leading mob family. Although they seemed to lived modestly, they built great wealth over generations through their illegal activities. It was a violent and difficult show, but one facet of it applies to our lesson. This mob family made their real living extorting "protection" money from hard-working people. In Judges, along with the servitude God's people were rendering, a common "tribute" payment was necessary on a regular basis. This could be viewed essentially as a tax, but it also served as protection money. Protection against whom? Not so much against outside invaders. Not so much against their fellow tribesmen or Israelites. No—this protection was from the ruling nation itself, Eglon, and the people of Moab. In other words, those who invaded said, "Pay us and we won't attack you. And while we're at it, we'll keep you safe from the neighbors, too."

How had Israel gotten into this fix? And what are the implications for us today? Henry David Thoreau is credited with saying, "The price of anything is the amount of life you exchange for it." In a world of conquest, nations took their eyes off their freedom at a perilous price. Their practical needs sometimes took precedence over such freedom. They needed to work, enjoy life, and be healthy. In Israel's case, they were also called to be faithful to God.

Any of us can give our time, attention, and resources to a pursuit or two. While few things may seem inherently bad, consider what happens when we become obsessed. We begin to jettison other important causes so that we can focus on our pursuit of the obsession. Verse 7 states the problem this way: "the people of Israel did what was evil in the sight of the LORD." We are not always given exact details of the evil they did, but among the charges here is worship of foreign gods. Verse 8 is plain in stating that the anger of God was kindled against Israel, so God "sold them into the hand of Cushan-rishathaim," who was the king of Mesopotamia. Their mental and spiritual enslavement to their obsessions transferred to literal servitude of the foreign king.

We cry out to God when we are in pain, just as the people do in verses 9-10. God gives Othniel as the deliverer who won their freedom in armed conflict. After forty years of peace, though, their attention wandered again. A new generation found ways to be distracted by other gods. They lost their freedoms and possibilities once more to enslavement at the hands of Moab (vv. 12-14). Again, eight years of servitude was their steep price.

Read Judges 3:15-30.
This passage describes the arrival of the time to pay the tribute. God sensed the sufferings of Israel under the occupation by Moab. Ehud

Ehud: Deception by a Lefty

of Gera came forth, raised up by God in response to the cries of the despondent people. Perhaps his rise was punctuated by his role in representing Israel in the delivery of the tribute. He seems to have built some rapport with the king.

Names are important here. Ehud is a *Benjamite.* In Hebrew, *Benjamin* seems to translate the phrase "son of the right hand" likely referring to the honored and much sought-after right hand—that is, the seat of favor near one who is in charge. Benjamin was a favored son. This theme of favored position is mentioned from time to time throughout the Old and New Testaments. For example, the brothers James and John asked Jesus if they might each sit next to him in his kingdom, one on the left and the other on the right. In Hebrews 12:1-2, readers are encouraged to run the race with endurance and focus, keeping an eye on Jesus who has endured and is now seated at the right hand of the throne of God.

In Scripture, the right hand indicates a favored position. But this is a bit tricky. Ehud is the "son of the right hand," but he turns out to be left-handed. What are the odds? And his left-handedness will play a key role in the story. At some point not described in this text, Ehud has decided that this is the time to act. His name will not be the only portrait of the deception he will use to win the freedom of Israel. He has a long dagger made, a *two-edged sword.* There is an allusion here to the two-edged nature with which Ehud's words will soon cut Eglon.

These details are important to the story. If you have already read the entire text for today, you know that Ehud being left-handed helped him to conceal his weapon and gain the element of surprise. Rick Hogaboam points out that Ehud's attack is given stealth by his being left-handed. Their concern for a weapon would likely have been focused on where a right-handed person would keep a knife or dagger. There may not have been an inkling that Ehud's concealed weapon was simply hiding on the other side.

Next, another quirky detail comes to the surface. His name appears to have roots in the Hebrew word for "baby bull" or "calf" and is normally used to connote something or someone who is round.

In many eras and cultures, a stout physical stature has represented affluence and wealth. Eglon's size makes him an oddly-shapen target that is almost comical, if not for the obvious violence. Although we may understand him to be a literally obese person, we should also interpret the mention of his size as a symbol of the world's injustice.

He is portrayed as a "fat cat," one who has benefited excessively by taking advantage of other peoples' sweat and suffering.

Ehud uses a bit of deception in verse 15-23. He lies to Eglon so he can get a private audience with him, and this private audience will allow him to carry out the murderous hit. Perhaps he has even worked to build trust with Eglon over time with just such a day in mind. This is his chance to assassinate the king in order to gain Israel's freedom. The defeat of this leader would signal the end of Moab's rule over the smaller, weaker people.

Anyone who is squeamish may want to skip this part. For Ehud carries out his attack, and Eglon's considerable girth conceals the wound, so deep does the small sword go. If the baby bull or calf motif is continued, then Eglon represents a fatted-killing that portends an important occasion for Israel. They are now delivered through his having been offered up. Maybe we are told that Eglon is fat and that his dung comes out for powerful reasons.

What might the reasons be for such graphic detail? As we see what is physically inside Eglon now come outside, we note that it is dirty waste—a powerful symbol of the way this overbearing ruler is to be viewed. He is one who has oppressed and taken advantage of the people of Israel. Rather than good inside him, there is darkness and dirt, which is now displayed for all to see. Who among us can read this text and not connect powerfully with that kind of symbolism? We too keep much hidden inside us. The world cannot see what we keep in our innermost being. When God is allowed access, though, there is no hiding. What is inside us may as well be outside, for God sees with eyes that miss no secrets.

Escape and Victory

What ensues beginning in verse 24 grows almost comedic, even in its darkness. For as Ehud escapes out the back door, the king's guards begin to question the amount of time that has passed since they saw him. This scene begs for a playwright or a screen portrayal. Picture the guards, shuffling back and forth on each foot. They steal a glance at one another. Perhaps they murmur. On the one hand, they feel as though they should check on the king. On the other, they do not wish to incur the wrath of wrongly intruding.

The door is locked. Perhaps they knock, first softly and then more loudly. We hear mention that the king might be in the bathroom for a significant amount of this time. They do not wish to disturb such a private moment. Sadly for them, their deliberation only serves to give Ehud more time to escape. Their indecision puts more distance between the Israelite assassin and their now dead ruler.

Ehud moved along without anyone being the wiser, and without being harmed. We should notice that verse 26 mentions the idols he runs past on his way. They are the closest Ehud comes to having witnesses to his deed, yet they cannot speak. They will not tell his story. He has defeated a crooked ruler, and the gods that ruler served. We do well to remember that potential gods beckon all around—gods that would tempt us to give them power over us! Ehud's story reminds us that they have no power to give.

The Cycle Starts Again

The land is given rest for "eighty years" (v. 30). This rest won't last forever because Israel will once again break covenant. Another judge will be needed, and more will rise to lead after that. Later, kings will rule Israel. As for Ehud, his performance and vision showed him to be a stabilizing force in Israel. For his lifetime, the people of Israel once again seemed to be in charge of their own resources.

1. Is anyone in the group left-handed? How is life different for left-handers in our culture?

_____

_____

_____

_____

_____

2. When people say, "Well, she's a sweetheart, but she just can't stay out of her own way," what kind of observation are they usually making? What patterns have they probably seen in the individual they are discussing?

_____

_____

_____

_____

_____

3. Read Hebrews 12:1-2. What do these verses seem to offer Christians in contrast to the patterns of distraction and enslavement we see in Judges?

_____

_____

_____

_____

_____

4. It seems that the heroic act in this story is the murder of Eglon. How does the murder of a human being fit with God's larger purposes?

_____

_____

_____

_____

_____

5. What did you connect with most powerfully in this story?

_____

_____

_____

_____

_____

6. What purpose do you believe this story serves in the larger biblical picture? Discuss this with your group.

_____

_____

_____

_____

_____

7. One central theme is that what was inside Eglon was finally exposed for all to see. How can you relate that to the living of your own life?

_____

_____

_____

_____

_____

8. False gods are the only witnesses to Ehud's escape after his brave act. What meaning do you draw from that?

_____

_____

_____

_____

_____

Deborah Lights a Fire and Jael Drives a Stake

Judges 4:1-24

A Cautionary Parable

There once was a man who had been coddled as a child. His home was a wealthy one! Any problem he created was quickly solved by his parents. There was no mess too large for their ability to clean up and no corner they were unwilling to cut so they could see their boy happy. This way of living was reinforced within him. As he grew up, he expected not to worry about how much effort or integrity was required in life. Instead, his only expectation was that things should work out in his favor. Pleasure and entertainment were his goals, for the less romantic sides of life had not been his burden.

Over time, he found himself less and less a part of the world around him. Having seen much and possessed of almost everything, he began to feel cut off from people around him. No matter, for he continued to run over whomever he must to gain the desires of his heart. Besides, he thought, they were inferior to him anyway. If he could want something—anything—how bad could that thing be? So his pursuits continued.

Later in life, his parents were gone. Also gone were the friends, neighbors, and colleagues whom his parents had leaned on. He was affluent, but he was also surrounded by those who would benefit from what they could steal from him. And he was devoid of allies. More and more of his time went into keeping what he had. He did not notice his own decline in health, and no one was there to point out where he was vulnerable from his excesses. He didn't know his blind spots. One by one, those who would take advantage of him learned ways in which to do so.

He did not even notice when some of what he owned began to be depleted. He did not realize how closely his detractors had moved into his life. In small parts, his world shrank. By the time he was old, this once strong and wealthy man was broke and timid. Asked to describe what had happened to him, one observer said, "His folks taught him every trick in existence—except the ability to stay out of his own way. He eventually devoured himself." What does this cautionary parable teach us? The so-called Judge's Cycle illustrates how a people who possessed a rich land could repeat a pattern of self-destruction and lose everything they cherished.

Consequences of Bad Choices

Think back. Silently, or in the trusted discussion of your group, think about one decision that you wish you had made differently. In other words, if you could go back and choose again, which decision would you make in a different way?

In our last session, we learned that the judge Ehud won a victory over King Eglon through boldness and trickery. With Ehud as a judge, the land was said to be at peace for the rest of Ehud's life. There is a single mention of a leader called Shamgar (3:31) under whom there was said to be peace after he won a great victory. Some believe variously that this verse's mention of an ox-goad signals either an underground effort against the Philistines or a surprise attack featuring the use of an innovative, pointed, spear-like instrument.

Read Judges 4:1-3.
In any event, the people eventually lapsed into independence from God and suffered the consequences: "And the LORD sold them into the hand of Jabin king of Canaan, who reigned in Hazor; and the commander of his army was Sisera, who lived in Harosheth-hagoyim. The sons of Israel cried to the LORD; for he had nine hundred iron chariots, and he oppressed the sons of Israel severely for twenty years" (4:1-3). In Old Testament terms, this was viewed as God's punishment or discipline of the Israelites. Since God's greatest work has always been to redeem and draw humanity nearer, the intent was to awaken them, transform them, and turn them away from their destructive path before they once again damaged themselves.

When we read this text through a New Testament filter, we might see the people simply receiving the just payment for what they had sown (Gal 6:7). The Israelites had chosen to distance themselves from God by the ways they lived. We are rarely told of specific sins in Judges. Unlike the prophets, who name specific offenses, Judges gives us a larger perspective rather than details.

God sold (v. 2) them into the hands of Jabin. The word (*mawkar* in Hebrew) that most of our Bibles translate as "sold" can also mean "surrender." In other words, we can surmise that God allowed them in their vulnerability, distractedness, and spiritual distance to be overtaken. Jabin took Israel under his rule and oppressed them for twenty years. More important for our purposes, his primary instrument of oppression was the army commander Sisera.

Verse 3 mentions that the people cry out once again. There is a painful, sobering reminder here about bad choices. Early in our story, the Israelites repented. We get the idea that they turned predictably back toward God. They wished to be redeemed and rescued from the pain of oppression. The problem is that a mighty army stood in their way. Their opponent was real. And now there is no quick fix for the wreckage left behind. That is the nature of our own sin or distractedness. Long after we realize our shortcomings, the consequences are still there.

Deborah's Many Hats

Read Judges 4:4-9.

Verses 4-5 say, "Now Deborah, a prophetess, the wife of Lappidoth, was judging Israel at that time. She used to sit under the palm tree of Deborah between Ramah and Bethel in the hill country of Ephraim; and the sons of Israel came up to her for judgment." Her role was not unusual in that time within ancient Israel, but there are not always specific names attached to this local or regional leadership task. Deborah emerges as one of the few stated examples of what we assume a "judge" was there to do. The people came to air their issues and to have their disputes settled.

Deborah's name comes from a Hebrew word whose root might mean "bee," a stinging insect. On the other hand, some of the same consonants found in the Hebrew root for "to speak" or "word" are also found in the Hebrew word for Deborah. It is possible that her role as prophetess is being portrayed in her name—or even that her words brought a stinging touch of reality to her people, typical of the prophets God raised up.

However, let us not overlook the other descriptor. Deborah was the *wife of Lappidoth*, as some translations render this phrase. It can also be translated "woman of torches" and may have nothing to do with her husband. When we consider her leadership, the second understanding may be more likely. She might have led her people into battle, for instance, by carrying a torch for the soldiers to follow.

Deborah served God in a variety of roles. She shared the perspectives and teachings of God as a prophetess, and she led as a judge. We will see her out front in military efforts. Finally, she was a wife (5:7). She must have had a lot of character to be able to serve God in so many important roles. Brian Harbour notes that Deborah fills four roles in her community: prophet, judge, military leader, and wife and mother. Doing so "underscores her significance" among biblical characters (61).

Here is the point at which some believers cheer for Deborah. What admirable qualities! But rather than anoint her as a hero, what if we chose to learn from her? God has placed certain gifts and abilities in our lives and gives us opportunities to hone the raw materials of those gifts and abilities. We are tested and stretched. We are challenged and taught. If we are near God, we can look back and see how God worked in our lives along the way. Deborah did more than one would think possible in God's kingdom, but her availability and closeness to God are simply the starting places for application of this story. We can be close to God and are called to do so. We can be available to God, uniquely gifted, and are called to do so. Let us not merely admire Deborah. Let us be challenged by her.

In verses 6-8, we learn that Deborah

> sent and summoned Barak the son of Abinoam from Kedesh-naphtali, and said to him, Behold, the LORD, the God of Israel, has commanded, "Go and march to Mount Tabor, and take with you ten thousand men from the sons of Naphtali and from the sons of Zebulun. I will draw out to you Sisera, the commander of Jabin's army, with his chariots and his many troops to the river Kishon, and I will give him into your hand. Then Barak said to her, if you will go with me, then I will go; but if you will not go with me, I will not go."

Have you ever said "maybe" to God? Perhaps you struggle to recall an exact instance where that word was your reply, but don't we live a "maybe" by our hesitancy or lack of effort? Don't we gridlock ourselves by hoping for a perfect opportunity? Deborah did go, but she assured Barak that God would hand Sisera over into the hand of a woman (v. 9).

The Canaanite Defeat

Read Judges 4:10-16.

Barak called together 10,000 men to fight. They came from various tribes and regions. Others sat out the call to battle. Sisera was armed in a way superior to the Israelites. This is especially portrayed by the detail that he had 900 chariots made of iron (v. 13). Deborah proclaimed the day of these armies' meeting as a day in which God would deliver to Israel the victory over Sisera and the Canaanites. A great battle ensued, and Israel's strength proved sufficient. When have you felt that you were too weak for the situation ahead? When has your church appeared to lack something vital with which to fulfill the calling of God? You have been tired, but God has seen you through. You have lacked, but God has provided enough—perhaps in ways that proved different from what you expected, but God was out front leading. In the end, Barak and Deborah led Israel in defeat of Canaan's might.

How unlikely is it that Barak's army of Israelites would wind up chasing Sisera's mighty army? The enemy's armored and heavily fortified chariots were reduced to vehicles of escape. What a turn of events! How long has it been since you allowed God to surprise you? What does your list of *impossible* feats for God look like?

This section ends with a stark picture: Sisera leaves his chariot and runs on foot to escape. This great army leader is humbled by the ragtag and fractious people who have been revitalized by God. He eventually runs for shelter and right into trouble.

Jael Joins Deborah and Barak

Read Judges 4:17-24.

Verse 17 leads us into the final defeat of Sisera. From here to the end of our text, the details are vivid. We meet Jael, another powerful female in this chapter. She turns out to be instrumental in Sisera's defeat and, by extension, the defeat of Canaan. But she did not have to run onto the field of battle to join the fight. Sisera ran into her tent.

Jael appears to have been a nomad. Perhaps this factor put Sisera at dangerous ease. Whatever he thought he found in her, this woman's friendliness hid her initiative. She had perspective about who Sisera and his army were: Maybe she sensed God's hand upon Israel and responded with insight and wisdom. In one deceptive welcome and in one surprising blow, Jael stopped the great oppressor of Israel for good.

Critics respond in a variety of ways when debriefing Jael. Some say she was attuned to the side and cause of Israel. Others say she was grounded enough to root out the evil and oppression that Sisera bore. Still others say her cleverness was as evil and dangerous as Sisera's threat. Anyone who could feign hospitality and turn it into a murderous ambush must be a dangerous character.

God's ability—and habit—of using unexpected characters to perform necessary acts is striking. We might consider that God, our sovereign Creator, moves among whomever God chooses. God redeems and recasts, empowers and moves forward with any people necessary!

1. How might a woman have risen to such prominence in male-dominated ancient Israel as Deborah did?

_____

_____

_____

_____

_____

2. If you step back and look at your service to God, how many "hats" do you wear? How do you try to serve God in each area?

_____

_____

_____

_____

_____

3. When have you felt unprepared, or shy of resources, for the calling you clearly hear from God? How have you tended to react in those moments?

_____

_____

_____

_____

_____

4. In the cautionary parable that begins our study, the man's own indulgences "devoured" him. Is there a bad decision in your past that you wish you could go back and redo? How might things be different if you could?

_____

_____

_____

_____

_____

5. Even in their repentance, the people of Israel still faced the consequences of their earlier way of life. The army of Sisera stood in front of them and took them over. What are we to do with this cautionary tale?

_____

_____

_____

_____

_____

6. Deborah and Barak are vastly outnumbered in this text. When have you felt too weak or ill equipped for something God was calling you to do? What did you do? What did God do?

_____

_____

_____

_____

_____

7. What does God's use of Jael teach you personally? How do you view God's capacity for surprise and creativity in achieving divine purposes?

_____

_____

_____

_____

Gideon, Part 1: Don't Be Mad at Me, God

Session   *Judges 6:25-40*

Read Judges 6:25-40.

As you go through life, do you find yourself accumulating questions? I do. Someone recently proposed a few of life's funnier curiosities.

1. If laughter is the best medicine, why do some people say they *die* laughing?
2. Why do people say "heads up" when they really mean you should duck?
3. Why do doctors leave the room when you change? They're going to see you naked anyway.
4. Why is it that when we "skate on thin ice," we can "end up in hot water"?
5. Why is the Lone Ranger called "Lone" if he always has Tonto with him?

Well, these may not be *the* most pressing questions you have, but they can trouble us.

If we are paying attention, our session text should alert us to something troubling. And it raises a more imponderable question than those we heard earlier: if we are not supposed to approach God by extending a test, then why does Gideon get away with it? And if Gideon did, will I?

In the Bible, God tells the people *not* to test the Almighty. In the Pentateuch, Deuteronomy 6:16 reads, "Do not test the LORD your God as you did at Massah." Massah is one of many examples in the Israelites' journey from Egypt to the promised land in which the people cried out to God, actively doubting and questioning, "Is the LORD among us or not?" (Exod 17:7). It was at this point that

God gave them water from a stone. Looking back on this experience, God warned the people through Moses: "Why do you put the LORD to the test?" (Exod 7:2).

And there are other biblical writings that should cause us discomfort over what Gideon does in Judges, like James 1:5-7: "If any of you lacks wisdom, he should ask God, who gives generously to all without finding fault, and it will be given to him. But when he asks, he must believe and not doubt, because he who doubts is like a wave of the sea, blown and tossed by the wind."

Jesus himself said on two occasions that it is "a wicked and adulterous generation that seeks after a sign" (Matt 12:28; 16:1-4).

In Judges 6:25, Gideon receives a calling from the Lord to destroy his own father's altar to Ba'al. Obviously, this is compelling because of the family entanglement. On the one hand, Gideon's calling is coming from God. But this is his father's property and practice. If Gideon were to violate the local Ba'al altar that his family is maintaining, he could place all of them in a vulnerable, even dangerous position.

Then again, God's angel has forecast that Gideon is a "mighty warrior" (v. 12). That is, he is a man of valor, and God will be with him—even unto victory over oppression.

The Midianites were keeping their thumbs on Gideon's tribe. We don't know much about the Midianites, although they appear to have been a powerful and nimble nomadic desert tribe outside the contested bounds of Israel. They made periodic raids and generally kept the Hebrew settlers scared. They lived off the hard work of Gideon's people, taking what was not theirs because no one seemed able to stop them.

The humble families of Israel subsisted on what they could raise up out of the land. If they had surplus, they sold their goods at market. The problem was that they had taken to living in caves and hillsides, sneaking down to their own properties in fear. The Midianites and Amalekites, among others, were marching through and plundering the Israelites' crops before the harvest, and Gideon's people appeared powerless against them.

Today, we would call this bullying. Today, we would call this thievery.

Emboldened by what he heard from God, Gideon mustered the courage to give the new plan a try. Why not pull down the altar and destroy it? Lest we forget, Gideon himself has been more acquainted with the practices of Ba'al worship than Yahweh worship. So his obedience to God should strike us as remarkable. Predictably, the surrounding powers march to strike Gideon's people and stamp down this small rebellion.

As God calls him to action in chapter 6, Gideon protests in a way reminiscent of Moses. He reminds God that his tribe is weak and that he is from the lowest family within that tribe. He is no one, or so he thinks. God thinks otherwise.

We finally see Gideon rise up and obey God in our text. The townspeople call out Joash, Gideon's father, to offer up his son to die for the act of rebellion in taking down Ba'al. The reaction by Gideon's father, in solidarity with his son, is remarkable. Joash poses a test: if Ba'al is much of a god, then let him contend for himself (see v. 31). But the altar to Ba'al lies in ruins. Gideon's father essentially joins forces with his son and calls the people back to recognizing the one true God, Yahweh.

What can we learn from that reaction? That is, if what I have awarded power in my life is really the god I think it is, then let it sustain itself. Let it rule. Let it demonstrate its validity. And then, in the face of mounting evidence that my latest god might not be sufficient, maybe I should reconsider.

What happens next is compelling. The bullies come to town. They want to inflict some punishment. Midianites, Amalekites, and unidentified others arrive and camp out, showing their great power and numbers. However, God has promised Gideon that victory can be his. Gideon gets the word out to a number of groups. Tired, oppressed people decide they have had enough and show up to march with Gideon. Gideon's interesting reaction takes place in verse 36.

Some have reacted to the action in Judges 6 by observing that what Gideon did was the same as tossing a coin in the air and saying, "All right God. Heads, I'll do this your way say; tails, I won't." And then, after God met that test, contrary to all biblical wisdom, Gideon said, "Okay, God, how about best two out of three?" In other words, the story does not seem to be about Gideon "testing" God to see what God's will or direction was. Gideon was already clear on that. It may be more about Gideon deciding whether or not he was going to comply with God's direction.

This might make us a little uncomfortable. What else can we learn in this episode? What does Gideon have to teach us?

God Decides How to React to Us

Gideon does something that I wouldn't advise you or me to do: he tests God, and not once but twice. Even so, God worked with Gideon because God will move where God wishes to move. We need that reminder from this text.

Each of us has a *box* that we make to contain the Almighty. We know what God looks like. We know what God sounds like. We know who God likes. We know what politicians and political decisions God supports. We know what God cares about and who God cares about, including which team God roots for. We know how God does things. Pretty soon, we leave no room for the surprises of God. There isn't eyesight to see or hearing to listen when God deviates from what we expected.

Gideon's story can puzzle us in some ways. Had I been there, I would have counseled Gideon to react differently to the visit by the angel of God. In my work, I watch a lot of people put God to the test. I am not comfortable with that approach. How do you feel about it?

Do not test the Lord thy God! we hear in our spirits. But we have to admit that, in the end, only God is in charge of how God will react to us.

Moses and Abram (later Abraham) are prominent characters in the Old Testament narrative. Each received a sign from God, but neither of them *requested* a specific sign. They did not test God as Gideon does in Judges 6 (v. 36). Moses got his sign as God spoke to him originally. Then, God told Moses what to do that would be a sign to help other people believe. Finally, God promised Moses one more sign, which he would get only *after* doing what God told him to do. Once Moses had completed his task, he would worship God on the very mountain on which he was standing.

Abram's sign from God was a promise: God told him that after he was dead he would get his sign. Abram's descendants would be slaves in a foreign land for 400 years. Then, they would be freed for use by God as a holy people. God even gave him a new name: Abraham. This man through whose seed the Lord chose to save the whole world never saw his sign.

Some have suggested that Gideon's story might be different because *God* called upon *Gideon*—and Gideon wasn't close to God at the time. He probably didn't know a better way to respond to God. Unlike Gideon, I *am* supposed to know better. But I have to admit that at times I don't. This text comforts me in an odd way because I am reminded that God knows what to do in the times when I don't!

God is in charge of responding to us. We want to understand Gideon's story through our own experiences and through our own theology. Instead, we need to know God on God's terms.

When God Calls, God Will Provide

I firmly believe that God will provide. I have staked my life in vocational ministry on that belief. I would not be doing what I do if I did not believe in God's provision and sufficiency.

Why should any of us trust in God? Because God has a track record. God has been enough for a lot of people before our time. God has given enough. God has done enough. And we trust that God will do still more! But let's be honest. Gideon was being asked to believe very deeply in a God he was not altogether familiar with.

In the space of four short years, America was dealt humbling blows in two separate incidents. You may remember where you were as you heard the news of the terrorist attacks of September 11, 2001. Video images of the Twin Towers collapsing were shown again and again on the news. We watched, not quite able to believe the enormity of it at first. Then, in August 2005, we watched in horror as Hurricane Katrina devastated the Gulf Coast. Once again the images of loss and despair were difficult to believe all at once—thousands dead and tens of thousands displaced in an epic disaster.

These two events—September 11 and Hurricane Katrina—show us the scope of tragedy in that the first was a man-made disaster and the second occurred naturally. When disasters strike, we join Gideon in not quite believing the hand of God is on our shoulders. We seek clarity when the call comes that nudges us to be useful for God's causes. When we are encouraged to believe that God is at work, we may long for a sign.

Gideon had to work hard in order to believe. In fact, I'm not sure that all the signs and signals did that much for him. What seemed to make the biggest difference was jumping in and being a part of what God was doing. The same was true of Moses and Abraham, who also learned that God's best and most obvious signs are often visible long after the call to follow and obey.

One young minister advised another, even younger minister this way. He said, "You can't wait until you're totally ready. Sometimes you have to jump in and paddle as hard as you can. And trust God to do the rest!" When God calls, God will provide. But we'd better be careful. Because God will call.

God Is Patient

After his initial call to lead, Gideon responded by acting on trust. God told him to pull down the altar to Ba'al that was on his father's farm and to build a new altar to God—Yahweh—in its place. Then he was to worship God. So he did. The townspeople didn't like this. They had become so comfortable with Ba'al worship that the idea of pledging themselves to another God scared them.

As chapter 6 flows into chapter 7, we see that Gideon was committed to God. He didn't know exactly how the situation would play out. You and I don't either. He didn't know what the costs of following God's calling were going to be. You and I don't either.

Gideon's tests of God involved leaving a fleece out overnight. But there's more. What he did was to be honest before God. He even asked God to be *patient* with him. Actually, he asked God not to get *angry* with him. He really asked permission to be honest with God. And he asked for the help he needed. Verse 40 says something beautiful: "And God did so that night." Gideon's request was granted.

When was the last time you stood before God so honestly—so unedited and completely unscripted—that you felt the need to ask God's patience? In your uncertainty, have you called on God lately? In your fright, have you called on God lately? In your pain, frustration, confusion, or even anger, have you called on God lately?

People who have been to the bottom only to find it firm have called on God. People who have spoken honestly have found God willing to listen. People who have offered themselves to God but weren't exactly ready have found God to be quite patient.

Gideon's story will inspire some reflection. What are you giving God to work with? What are *we* giving God to work with?

1. What is the boldest thing you have ever done? What is the unlikeliest choice you have made against great odds?

_____
_____
_____
_____
_____

2. What are some things about life that you are curious about?

_____

_____

_____

_____

_____

3. What are some things about God—and about God's ways—that you wish you understood more?

_____

_____

_____

_____

_____

4. In Judges 6, what background helps us understand why God may have raised up Gideon as the next great leader of the people (see 6:1-32)?

_____

_____

_____

_____

_____

5. In this session's text, Gideon clearly puts God to a "test" of sorts. What is your reaction to this in light of your own beliefs about how God works?

_____

_____

_____

_____

_____

6. Why do you believe God appeared more patient or receptive in this episode with Gideon than in some other stories of the Bible?

_____

_____

_____

_____

7. What are some "boxes" you tend to put God in? In other words, what are some assumptions about God—and about what God would or would not do—that most powerfully shape your faith?

_____

_____

_____

_____

_____

8. What from this text might challenge some of the assumptions you have had about God?

_____

_____

_____

_____

_____

9. What from your life of faith helps you to believe that, when you don't know what to do, God does know?

_____

_____

_____

_____

_____

Beginning at the Beginning

Gideon's story is a rollicking adventure. This reluctant leader somehow emerges victorious against insurmountable odds. Does this premise sound clichéd? God went to great lengths in Gideon's story to assure that he was vastly outnumbered. Viewed conventionally, the battle Gideon was to lead was unwinnable. But a moment spent remembering where all of this started might help us.

My friend pastors a large and quite sophisticated church. I suspect one reason he appeals to his people is that he defies convention. In a medium-sized city, with a mostly upscale demographic to serve, my friend adds steady doses of insight from his farm upbringing. Don't get me wrong: He is cultured and intelligent. He is well educated. His congregation knows this. But they also love the variety and contrast he brings to their sometimes bland professional worlds.

Once, his blog heralded the safe arrival of some big and juicy tomatoes he grew. In previous years, he had encountered obstacles to his gardening. Drought killed off one year's crop. Another time, a bug infestation ruined it. Once, his tomatoes almost matured to ripe deliciousness when a deer sneaked in and devoured them. This year, though, he successfully fended off all dangers and was enjoying the fruits of his considerable labor. His work as a pastor is similar. He has faithfully tended the wisdom and talent God has given him. He is the right person for the right time.

As chapter 6 unfolded in the previous session, Gideon was out on the threshing floor in Ophrah. His frightened band of fellow Israelites was holed up in caves and hills. The Midianites and the Amalekites oppressed them, stealing the meager outcomes they managed to produce in the fields. Israel appeared powerless to stop the bullying. Imagine how demoralizing it would be to labor at a farm only to find that just as you were ready to sustain your family, outsiders would swoop in and pocket your goods. Over time, Israelites in this area adapted their lifestyles to hide and live in the higher grounds. Then they would sneak down to prepare their crops if they managed to bring them to full harvest.

Out of this strain and humiliation, Gideon is found working at his father's fields. A messenger of God comes to him and calls him to lead the Israelites in battle. God has noticed the plight of these beaten-down people. God has heard their cries and sensed their sorrow. The time has come for Israel to overturn their oppressors.

What qualities do you think might have caused God to choose Gideon? How might God determine who was fit to lead a group of people in such a dangerous and physical confrontation?

On the one hand, Gideon may have been physically strong. His stature may have made him stand out among his people as one who could make an effective warrior. Also, he might have had great leadership qualities. People could have followed Gideon locally. Among these needy people, his strength of body and mind may have made him a charismatic natural. Of course, this is speculation; we really do not know from the Scripture.

Later parts of Judges 7 might make us rethink our usual images. We tend to read Scripture with our assumptions in place. We are biased to think God would look for a strong, attractive, charismatic leader. After all, verse 12 shows the messenger referring to Gideon as a "mighty man of valor." But what if God had a point to make with the Israelites? As we will see demonstrated a few verses later, what if God approached this mission with a minimalist strategy, choosing a leader who was unconventionally small or not particularly strong? Maybe a quiet, bookish person. If you are feeling that this kind of story feels familiar, there is good reason. David and Goliath will feature some of the same dynamics, as God chooses again to call out an undersized hero.

There are many ways to be strong. Strength can take on a stereotypical bulk, but strength and endurance can also be packaged in other ways.

The 1993 film *Rudy* was a hit with those of us who love a good underdog story. This film has been voted to several "greatest" lists because it connected with what is core to our humanity. Based on the real-life story of Daniel "Rudy" Ruettiger, the movie portrays strength in a small package indeed. At 5'6" and 165 pounds, Rudy was not the kind of football player Notre Dame recruited. Along with size or talent, he also lacked the grades or the money to attend Notre Dame. Yet his dream to play there stayed with him. From his job at a local steel mill, he persisted and got his chance to be a walk-on with the team.

You have known other examples of unlikely strength. The husband who sits by his wife's side for a decade as her dramatic illness renders her alive but homebound. The parents who lack extra funds but who live frugally so their kids can have an education and a chance in life the parents never got. The young person who stays with his morals and convictions, especially at the expense of a "hip" social life he would have if only he were willing to compromise and go with the majority. A single mother who works at her menial job not just to survive but also to strive for her drug-addicted child's treatment and recovery.

These are the unlikely heroes that God watches over. A coworker once observed about a person we knew, "She's like that old country song. If it weren't for bad luck, she'd have no luck at all." Yet we celebrated that this person showed up every day at work with a dedication and outlook that we envied.

A Call to Win the Battle

Gideon had a specific call placed on his life. He was to lead the Israelites in an uprising against the Midianites and the Amalekites. Once he exchanged his doubts for God's assurance, Gideon plunged in. We ought to learn something from that.

On the other hand, we continue to sense his reticence throughout chapter 7. We modern Christians like our biblical characters bold and intentional! We probably prefer them to play like actors in a movie—everything scripted and assured before the filming ever starts. Rarely do we stop to consider that Gideon certainly had no script to go by. He didn't even have a leather-bound copy of Scripture to carry around and read. He was living this story in real time.

Variously, courage has been defined in helpful ways. Most versions seem to go like this: *Courage is not the absence of fear but the willingness to move forward anyway.* Or my favorite: *Courage is knowing what lies just around the corner and then making the turn anyway.*

If you read commentaries on this section of Judges, you will see a range of reactions. Some are tough on Gideon. They point out (rightly) that his faith was not all that great. He repeatedly tested God after what should have been incontrovertible evidence. Yahweh's mighty presence had been demonstrated. However, we may rob these stories of at least one dimension of their power if we try to insist that Gideon should have been less hesitant.

For our purposes, I am going to suggest that we let Gideon be who the Bible portrays him to be. Rather than explaining away his tests of God, let's plumb them along with the rest of the story. Instead of ridiculing his uncertainties about God, let's match them with our own confessions of doubt.

Gideon Leads Out

Read Judges 7:1-8.
Once Gideon took action in chapter 6 by removing the Ba'al altar on his father's land, he was committed to the cause. Now, the rival armies are poised nearby. Other than running away, Gideon has no choice but to follow through.

We need to consider how hard we all grasp at God in an attempt to possess God. Perhaps unconsciously, we try to control God. Phillips Elliott asserts that once Gideon sensed God's legitimacy, he became a person possessed by God (736). That is, Gideon has been a rather novice devotee to God, but we watch an evolution taking place here. Jesus echoed this dynamic in John 15:16 as he urged the disciples to a similar level of faith experience: "You have not chosen me, but I have chosen you, and ordained you that you should go and bring forth fruit." We see in the Gospels that the followers of Jesus were not fully strong or independent. They did not demonstrate a consistently developed theology.

Gideon leads his followers to the spring of Harod, just below Mount Gilboa. The Midianite encampment is north of them. Gideon's army consists of 32,000 souls who are tired enough of the oppression to fight in rebellion. In an odd move, God chooses to point out that there might be too many soldiers to take up the battle. Judges 8:10 will later number the opposing forces at 120,000, so the Israelites already sound grossly under prepared. What is God doing?

In 7:2-3, Gideon prepares his troops in a manner consistent with Deuteronomy 20:1-8. That is, he says that if any of them are fearful and trembling, they should go home. Just return to their people. We see that the result is that 22,000 of his troops take him up on the offer!

Unthinkably, God insists that this is still too many to fight. Verses 4-8 recount the infamous drinking water episode. The 300 who lap at the water from their hands (like dogs) are kept. All the others kneel to drink. Gideon does as the Lord requires and dismisses them.

A Most Curious and Lonesome Act

Read Judges 7:9-18.
What unfolds next is even odder than the campaign that has so drastically reduced Israel's army. The writer of Judges makes one thing clear: God is in no mood to risk the Israelite army taking military credit for the upcoming victory.

Have you ever sensed that God has worked an unthinkable act in your presence? Not just a warm and fuzzy act. Not simply a meaningful moment or a helpful insight. I am talking about an outcome or feat that cannot be understood without simply acknowledging God's work. When we know that only God could have done whatever we have experienced, we are humbled. We are affected and changed. This was the kind of outcome God wanted for Israel at this point in their pilgrimage.

We see Gideon being sent alone right into the middle of the enemy encampment. There is a funny picture going around the Internet these days. A big fluffy cat is walking along with its tail in the air. It looks as though it has not a care in the world. But lined up beside the cat must be twenty German shepherds. The caption reads, "Yea, though I walk through the valley of the shadow of death, I will fear no evil." One can picture Gideon the same way. But Gideon is not being tested here. He is being shown a sign he didn't ask for. God wants to demonstrate to Gideon that victory lies ahead, but only through divine blessing and only to the faithful. It's a powerful reminder of Exodus 20:5: "I the LORD thy God am a jealous God."

Gideon is to go into the enemy camp at night. It is said that the combined armies of the Midianites and Amalekites lay sleeping along the valley like "locusts" (v. 12). We are to picture an overwhelming sight, with Gideon (and his servant Purah) walking right into the middle of them. Once there, he is simply to listen. What he hears is the telling and interpretation of a dream. The man has dreamed that "a cake of barley bread" tumbled into camp and flattened a Midianite tent. The enemies agree, in Gideon's hearing, that Israel has been handed the upcoming victory. Into Gideon's hand they will be delivered.

Notice that Gideon worships God then and there. This information gives him the courage to follow God's instructions further. From there, he returns to his own camp and assembles the army for God's victory.

Using mostly noise (vv. 20-23), his three companies of 100 men each confront the vast opposition. The combined armies of Midian and the Amalekites take to their feet and flee. So convinced are they that God is with Israel that, as other tribes are sent for, they continue their flight to the mountains and hillsides. Eventually, key leaders (princes) in Midian and other opposing provinces are killed by the Israelite soldiers. The people of Israel take back their territories and give up their fearful living.

Lessons in the Miracle

The lessons in this story are many. You can keep track of a list of your own insights. As we close, I will name a few takeaways that you might want to consider.

• God chooses whomever God wants to choose.
• God is always working toward an end desirable for humanity. Bullies will eventually be defeated and the oppressed will be encouraged.
• Those whom God uses may have to proceed despite not having all their questions answered. Or they may have to proceed despite not liking the answers they have received.
• While the Bible is clear that testing God is not the desired way to act on our wants, life with God will test us occasionally! In fact, life in general will mount up severe tests of our character, faith, and courage. Get ready.
• God will carry out what God wants to carry out, and often in unexpected ways. We do well to sense God's movement and stay out of the way.
• Like Gideon, we are not going to be finished products anytime soon. Instead, we serve God as works in progress. We participate despite our questions, our fears, and our lack of complete understanding.

What do *you* see in Gideon's story?

1. When you read miraculous stories in the Bible, how do you normally react? Do they help you connect with a teaching? Do they raise further questions?

_____

_____

_____

_____

_____

2. Do miracles in the Bible ever cause you to disconnect because they seem hard to relate to? Why? Why not?

_____

_____

_____

_____

_____

3. Why might God have wanted Gideon to use so few men for such a monumental task? Was there a larger lesson God wanted to teach? If so, what?

_____

_____

_____

_____

_____

4. What other biblical stories does this remind you of in which God used unlikely heroes or less-than-conventional approaches to do big things?

_____

_____

_____

_____

5. What qualities might Gideon have possessed that caused God to use him in this way? What qualities do you believe God most needs right now, today, to continue building the kingdom?

_____

_____

_____

_____

_____

6. God was working toward a hope for Israel. How would you describe the end toward which God is still working in our world today?

_____

_____

_____

_____

_____

7. Who are some of the least likely figures you have seen God work through in your lifetime? What can we learn from that?

_____

_____

_____

_____

_____

Abimelech: The Cost of Disloyalty and Greed

Do you tend to cry out to God more for rescue and relief? Or do you cry out to repair and restore your relationship with God? These are two very different reasons to lift an impassioned prayer to the Lord. Yet we do both these things. Maybe one of these is more your tendency than the other. Here are some words about the bumps and bruises of life:

• "Courage is fear holding on a minute longer." (George S. Patton, Jr.)
• "You may have a limp, but at least try to limp with a little panache!" (Jinny Henson)
• "Making the decision to have a child—it's momentous. It is to decide forever to have your heart go walking outside your body." (Elizabeth Stone)

The story of Abimelech may sound a little familiar. The son of a famous Israelite leader goes bad. He gets greedy and pushes for power. A struggle ensues and exacts tragic costs within the kingdom. Division and confusion result. A distracted people are led away from the relative calm and faithfulness of the father's era. Eventually, the son dies a painful death and fails to achieve the uppermost passion of his madness: the position of ruler.

There are similarities to the story of Absalom, whose well-known rebellion against his father David's throne plays out in 2 Samuel. That story takes place long after this family drama in Judges 9.

First, let's admit that Gideon did many things well! In a previous session, we watched him be used by God to lead his people out of oppression. They moved away from a mixture of idol worship and part-time attention to Yahweh to become more devoted to the Lord. Gideon led them while coming to faith in God himself since the idol he tore down was on his own family property. His battle against the Midianites had made him popular.

Near the end of Judges 8, we see a victorious Gideon approached by his men. They ask if he and his sons will lead them. He replies with exactly the right words: that he and his sons will not rule over the people but that God will be their ruler.

Then, in all-too-human fashion, Gideon turns around and builds a new altar to an idol. Having asked the people for a portion of the gold they took as spoils in the victory, he builds an "ephod" or sacred object from the gold. Although he has proclaimed the Lord the true ruler, the people travel from all around to worship this new idol at Ophrah. Confusion and divided allegiances break out, and the people begin a slow and steady departure from the emphasis on God that Gideon has pledged.

Abimelech's Rise to Power

Read Judges 9:1-6.
Abimelech was the half-son of Gideon by way of his concubine. Gideon had seventy sons by many different women. But this son was determined to rule on the heels of his father's popularity. He had no birthright, so he had to eliminate the legitimate heirs.

Judges 9 shows Abimelech going to his mother's clan at Shechem and asking them whether they would like to be ruled by the seventy sons of Gideon (or "Jerubbaal") who would reign from Ophrah or if they would rather the one son who was "your bone and your flesh" be their leader (v. 2).

With some campaigning, he won his cause. They gave him seventy pieces of silver, with which Judges says he went out and hired a band of followers. In fact, we read that they were "worthless and reckless fellows" (v. 4).

In short order, and without detail, we read that they slew the seventy sons of Gideon. Apparently, one battle led to another because Abimelech's youngest brother, Jotham—the only survivor—will speak on behalf of God.

The Curse of Jotham

Read Judges 9:7-21.

This passage shows Jotham protesting the people's toleration of Abimelech. He calls them out on their lack of judgment. Similar to Jesus' imagery of a fig tree that will not bear fruit, Jotham challenges the veracity of the people's direction. Meanwhile, Abimelech has had himself proclaimed "king" over all Israel. He rules for three years. J. Clinton McCann says that Judges 9 is, in short, "A portrayal of the disastrous results of Gideon's legacy" (71). Why so? Because Gideon reintroduced idol worship into the culture of Israel and left open the door for the people to choose their own gods. Rather than being faithful to the one true God, Yahweh, they freelanced and experimented with their own sense of fancy.

Perhaps worse, some scholars believe that Judges 9 serves a special purpose within the larger book. That is, after Gideon's time, the judges over Israel led the people even further away from God. As bad as things were in the eras we have studied, things were about to get even worse. Particularly, the bloody ending that is captured in chapters 17–21 seems set into motion here in Judges 9.

Shechem's Movement against Abimelech

Read Judges 9:22-45.

Gaal, son of Ebed (from the tribe of Ephraim) is brought in as the best hope the people have. He helps throw a big party and leads in a verbal uprising against Abimelech. Soon, the people of Shechem are organizing a revolt. A governor, Zebul, hears about this revolt. He delivers word to Abimelech. Abimelech gathers a group of soldiers and waits in the field for Gaal's men. There, they kill them.

Read Judges 9:46-57.

Then, Abimelech goes against the people of the city of Shechem, and, in a bloody, daylong battle, he overthrows the rest of the rebellion. This will be typical of the time after Gideon. When God is no longer ruling over Israel, someone else must be, and that someone will always be fighting to hold his place.

A final gathering at Shechem happens in the house of Elberith. The people of the Tower of Shechem are burned by Abimelech himself. From there, Abimelech goes to a nearby stronghold at Thebez. He hears of a large gathering there. As he draws near the tower wall at Thebez, a woman throws a portion of a millstone over the wall and hits Abimelech. The blow fractures his skull. He instructs his swordsman to kill him rather than have it told that he has been killed by a woman. A tragic ending among tragic endings.

Lessons from the Writer of Judges

• The calls to lead are sacred ones from God. When our ambition and greed move us to contrive a position that God might not attend, we can cause widespread and tragic consequences.

• We can say good words, but only if we follow them with the right actions do we give God the best to work with.

• God will often send a prophet to give voice against our excesses and our mistakes, but this only helps if we have ears to listen. In any event, God will speak to us—whether we heed God's voice or not.

• Decisions we make—and words we do not deliver on—can cause cascading ripples of tragedy that may be delivered upon future generations. Gideon's lack of conviction and practice may or may not have manufactured his particularly flawed son, Abimelech. But the ambivalence and naiveté that allowed Abimelech to take control of the people at Shechem—and consequently funded/empowered his reign of terror—must be partly laid at the feet of Gideon.

• Gideon could have been remembered only for his bravery and trust of God. Instead, because of his "wishy-washy" actions, he is remembered by many as "the flawed judge."

Pardon the sports analogy, but in baseball the runners put on base by a previous pitcher are "charged" to him if they score, even if the next pitcher is in the game when they do. The runners are charged to the record of the pitcher who allowed them to get on base in the first place. This chapter is ostensibly about Abimelech, but the tragic reality of this chapter is that Gideon's legacy is written instead. He was the one who allowed his son to get in this position in the first place.

In fact, much of the damage and downfall of Israel is about to be charged to Gideon's record.

1. What is the likeliest reason for you to stop and pray to God? What have you noticed about yourself in your prayers?

_____
_____
_____
_____
_____

2. Gideon refused to seize a conventional "ruler" role in Israel, despite the people pleading for him to do so. Instead, he proclaimed God as ruler of all. What are we to learn from this?

_____
_____
_____
_____
_____

3. What might have caused Gideon to build the idol altar that proved to be so popular?

_____
_____
_____
_____
_____

4. Sadly, Gideon's legacy is costly, some might say disastrous, for Israel. How so?

_____
_____
_____
_____
_____

5. Gideon's lack of consistency between his words and deeds caused a ripple through the next few generations. He set in motion a painful era. When have you observed this same pattern in families, cities, churches, or nations?

_____

_____

_____

_____

_____

6. To have been so heroic early on, Gideon emerged with the label of the "flawed" judge. Why would God have allowed this to be so? What can we learn from that?

_____

_____

_____

_____

_____

7. Does it seem fair or unfair to you that Gideon is remembered in this way? Why?

_____

_____

_____

_____

_____

8. Do you believe that God exercises too much control, too little control, or just about the right amount of control over our lives and choices? Explain your answer.

_____

_____

_____

_____

_____

Jephthah: Has God Had Enough?

Judges 10:6–11:28

Does God Turn Away from Us?

Do you believe it is possible that God can "have enough" with a person or a people? Based on your experience—and your knowledge of Scripture—mull that question over for a bit. On the one hand, many believe that the grace of God is boundless. Our Bible is a book of second, third, and fourth chances . . . and beyond. On the other hand, a text like this one reminds us that God can reach a place where moving on seems to be the only choice.

While we are pondering what we believe about God, let's consider one more question: do you believe that God can experience a change of mind? Or, in contrast, do you believe that the word and decisions of God are final? Again, Christians differ among each other on this question. For some, the mind of God is focused and disciplined. They would assert that God has no need for a mind change, since the will and knowledge of God are perfect. But a text like this one may challenge us on that too!

Read Judges 10:6-16.

Jephthah came along as the next noteworthy judge after Abimelech. Truthfully, there were two other judges immediately after Abimelech. However, we are given a grand total of five verses about Tola and Jair. Tola was the son of Puah. He came from Ephraim and judged for twenty-three years. He died, and we know little if anything else. The notion is that he was raised up by God and seems to have run an orderly operation, mostly owing to a lack of misdeeds or conflicts listed. Jair was from Gilead, and he judged Israel for twenty-two years. His story appears to connect with the Numbers 32:39-42 conquest of Gilead (Myers, 761). He is said to have had thirty sons who rode thirty donkeys, and they "had" thirty cities. This detail is given to indicate that Jair was wealthy. Again, that is all we know.

Jephthah was born during a time in which the children of Israel were once again living apart from God. The accusations are simple: They were worshiping foreign gods, and the list of the gods is long. From honoring Ba'al and Ashtaroth to following the gods of Zidon, Syria, Moab, Amnon, and the Philistines, the people of Israel are indicted for covering as many avenues as possible when it comes to worship. Not only were they following these gods, verse 6 tells us that they "forsook" Yahweh, the God of Israel.

Verse 7 tells us that "the anger of the LORD was hot against Israel, and he sold them into the hands of the Philistines and into the hands of the children of Ammon." By verse 10, we think we hear the familiar cry of Israel to God for delivery. But listen again. The children of Israel are in a particularly confessional mood. They get specific, noting first that they have forsaken God. Then, they confess to serving the Ba'als. God helps them along with their confession, reminding them in verses 11-12 of deliverance for which they should be thankful and that they should be living with a resultant loyalty. Instead, they have forsaken God (v. 13), and then we hear a harsh judgment.

God Will Save Them No More!

A ministry friend of mine tells a story from his college years. His father owned a tire shop in a small South Georgia town. My friend grew up and went off to college to get the education that his parents had always dreamed of providing. However, he didn't appreciate the opportunity as much as he should have. His lack of focus and effort resulted in an academic dismissal at the close of his freshman year. He called his father with the bad news and with the request that his dad help him move back home. The next day, his dad's truck pulled up to the dorm. My friend waited for the lecture to happen. He waited for the impassioned, frustrated, and loud voice of his dad's anger. Instead, he said the three-hour drive home was silent. His dad did not speak a word. The next morning, his dad told him to get ready for work. For the next three months, my friend worked in the stifling heat of the re-tread room in his dad's tire shop. The labor was hard and the misery oppressive. Only at the end of the summer did his dad finally address school again. He said, "Son, I talked to the people over at the university. They tell me that they will accept you back on a probationary status. You know, if you want another crack at that education . . . and at the next forty-five years of your life that don't include summers in my re-tread shop." My friend eagerly accepted. He earned his degree there, went right to seminary for his master's degree, and eventually earned a doctorate! Grace should always surprise and humble us. But, can God run out of patience permanently? People surely can.

We are treading new ground in Judges. In 10:13, God says that the people have been rescued for the last time. This is a stark departure from the grace-filled reaction God has had to their cries. But there is more. This time God recommends that Israel turn to their adopted gods for deliverance and help in the face of the oppression and suffering at the hands of the neighboring peoples (v. 14). "Talk to those gods for a while," Yahweh says. One can imagine just how quiet the lack of response and help might have been if the people had played along. Instead, we can hear the deafening sound of God's frustration.

In verse 15, we hear a different response from the Israelites than what they usually do. This time, the message to God seems to include a rather open-ended clause. That is, they tell God to do whatever God wants to do with them—but they beg God not to leave them another day in the misery of their present circumstances.

Misery not only likes company, it usually needs relief. Here in our story, the wages of their life's indulgences had brought a heavy price. The Rev. Jerry Clower used to tell a story about two squirrel hunters. One day, they went out and separated and found places to wait for their prey. One of them climbed a tree. About the time his friend came walking along down below, the man up in the tree got a big surprise. A squirrel climbed up his pants leg. The hunter felt the squirrel and grabbed around his shin to keep the animal from climbing any higher. Of course, this caused the squirrel to bite him. Lots of commotion ensued! The hunter would not turn the squirrel loose for fear he would go the wrong direction. The squirrel would not quit biting because he was trapped. The friend on the ground felt helpless because he had no way to stop this from happening, and he was scared his friend would fall out of the tree. The hunter yelled down to his friend, "Shoot him! Shoot him!" To which the friend replied that he was nervous to pull the trigger. He might hit his friend's leg instead of the squirrel. "Shoot him! Pull the trigger!" "But what if I hit you?" the friend begged. "That's okay—shoot him. Shoot me. One of us needs some relief!"

"Do to us whatever seems good to you; only deliver us, we pray, this day," the people tell God in verse 15. Have you ever felt this way, either spiritually or emotionally? Have you cried out to God, praying for help that you would pay almost any price to get?

Israel puts away the foreign gods they have been worshiping. We read in verse 16 that they served the Lord. God feels "indignant" (RSV) over the misery Israel is living in.

Read Judges 10:17-18.

Chapter 10 closes with an introduction to the Ammonite occupation of Gilead. Up to this point, we have heard a lot of names called in relation to *who* plays a part in Israel's hardship. But we know next to nothing about *what* is happening. What were these oppressive forces doing to God's children that caused so much sorrow? We have not known until now. Now, the Ammonites specifically are closing in like a bully on a smaller, weaker victim.

In verse 18, we read that the people are wondering aloud who will come and lead them into battle. Who will help them fend for themselves and drive away these unwelcomed brutes? That is the issue as we move into chapter 11.

Jephthah Is Petitioned to Lead

Read Judges 11:1-11.

In verses 1-11 of chapter 11, we see the people of Gilead approach Jephthah. In the background, we see that his status within his own family has rendered him somewhat of an outcast. His birthright and place are not as pure as that of his brothers, but they seem to know he is a mightier warrior than any of them. Awkwardly, they will drive him away and then plead with him when their time of need arrives. In his exile, Jephthah has apparently recruited (or at least drawn about him) a band of followers whose reputation was earned in toughness. So, naturally, Jephthah points out the inconsistency of their plea.

We expect our biblical characters to be as grace-filled as God. Somehow, we expect them to be different from us. We may be caught off-guard when they instead act vengeful or struggle with doing the right thing versus the convenient (or understandable or fair) thing. Jephthah replies in a way that initially disappoints us. But we may come to respect the way he stands up for himself.

In verse 9, Jephthah makes a deal. He proposes that if he does come home to lead Gilead in driving away their oppressors, and if he is successful in that effort, he should immediately become their leader. In verse 10, we see the elders acquiesce. They must feel that they have no one else from within to lead them. Suddenly, Jephthah moves from *persona non grata* to a welcomed returnee.

Jephthah Confronts the Opposition and Makes a Regrettable Vow

Read Judges 11:12-28.
We will see in this passage an attempt at diplomacy and bargaining between Jephthah and the king of the Ammonites. Jephthah tries to interpret Israel's conquesting history in light of God's sacred mandate. The king of the Ammonites seems to particularly begrudge the fact that Israel passed through his territory long ago without permission. Jephthah begs the understanding that Israel had asked for such permission and was not granted it. Still, their mandate from God was to move forward and occupy the land on the other side.

We struggle to see both sides. In our loyalty to the Israelite part of our Judeo-Christian heritage, we simply take God's mandate upon the "children" as a free pass for whatever they might do. In reality, we fail most times to consider how the neighboring and occupying peoples must have felt. Certainly, those who were dispossessed of their land by the conquest of Canaan had little good to say. And these groups across whose land Israel simply moved on the way to Canaan probably felt violated, too.

In any event, Jephthah and the king do not reach an accord.

Read Judges 11:29-40.
Jephthah now prepares for the inevitable battle. In verse 30, he swears that if God will simply empower him and bless Gilead for victory, he will sacrifice to and honor God. Specifically, he pledges that whatever first comes out of his own home's door will be given as a burnt sacrifice to God.

Battle ensues. In a one-verse summary, we hear that Jephthah did indeed win! Verses 32-33 say that the Lord delivered the Ammonites into his hand.

In verse 34, a victorious Jephthah returns home to Mizpah. Sadly, his daughter comes bounding out the door to meet him. She is in full celebration mode. Her festive dance includes timbrels! She is his only child. Jephthah immediately weeps and expresses his sadness. As chapter 11 ends, we see him living up to his word faithfully. He pays a steep price for a vow made leading to a war that should never have been fought in the first place.

Lessons from Jephthah

• Distraction and misspent attention to false gods will always pull us away from the real thing. Jesus reminded us that we could not serve more than one God at a time (Matt 6:24). Today, we speak of "multitasking," but there is beginning to be some cultural pushback at the notion. We cannot truly multitask; what we end up doing is dividing our fragile and finite attention span.

• Choose wisely when you invest yourself and your resources. The best you get might be the temporary enjoyment of your choice, even if time proves it is a poor one.

• Second chances may come. However, they will often come at great price. We may bargain away something precious in our negotiation. Or we may simply incur great cost as we go along fixing a situation that did not have to exist in the first place.

• "Never sacrifice the happiness of tomorrow on the altar of today!" (Prosser and Qualls, 1)

• Be very careful what you promise. Jephthah's "kept" promise to God somehow challenges us in an inspiring way once we recoil at the sacrifice of his young daughter. Nowhere does our Scripture suggest that God asked this sacrifice from Jepthah. Nor, that God demanded he keep his vow. Instead, we see a broken-hearted father choose to keep his word. This is disturbing. Why did he make such a vow in the first place? Yet, on some deep level his keeping of this horrifying vow is at least consistent and important enough to have been included in the scriptural story. We find ourselves bargaining with God. This seems to be what desperate believers do, yet Jesus instructed us to be sparing with our vows. He suggested that we simply say "yes, yes" or "no, no" (Matt 5:33-37). James 5:12 reiterates this very point in the quotable "Let your yes be yes, and your no be no."

1. Our study begins with the question *Can God turn from us?* What do you believe about this? Why?

_____

_____

_____

_____

_____

2. What do you make of the Bible's dual realities that, on the one hand, God can deal out what appears to be harsh punishment and then, on the other, can grant many "second" chances to the repentant. How do you sort all of this out?

_____

_____

_____

_____

_____

3. Can God change God's mind? Why do you believe so?

_____

_____

_____

_____

_____

4. In verse 15, we read, "Do to us whatever seems good to you; only deliver us, we pray, this day." Have you ever felt this way, either spiritually or emotionally? If so, what did God do?

_____

_____

_____

_____

_____

5. Jesus reminded us that we could not serve more than one God at a time. How does that apply to this story and others within the book of Judges?

_____

_____

_____

_____

_____

Jephthah: Has God Had Enough?

6. What do you think of the hard bargain Jephthah struck in this story? What can sometimes be the true cost of second chances?

_____

_____

_____

_____

_____

7. What does the saying, "Never sacrifice the happiness of tomorrow on the altar of today" have to do with our study?

_____

_____

_____

_____

_____

8. What do you think of a God who gives you freedom of choice but can also leave you to the consequences of your own choices?

_____

_____

_____

_____

_____

9. Why might God's way ultimately be the most loving arrangement with humankind?

_____

_____

_____

_____

_____

Samson: Strong and Smart
for a Purpose

Session

Judges 13:1-7; 16:4-31

We probably all know an overachiever; we may be one ourselves. Underdogs are people who aren't really given much and yet move on to greatness anyway.

• The student who grinds all the way through school and ends up with the same diploma the honor grad earned.
• The undersized athlete who gets the timely hits and overshadows the more publicized star when the games really count.
• The worker who is not among the company's elite recruits and who starts off low but then rises to upper management by the time her career ends.

Every family has one. Every school, church, and community has one, too.

Then, there was Samson. He was no underdog. You have to not be given much in order to earn that label.

Read Judges 13:1-7.
We read in the Scripture passage that Samson was made special for a purpose. Before he was even born, he was given gifts that seem to have defied convention. We know a few things about the context of this boy's birth:

• Israel had once again lapsed into distraction and weakness, and consequently they suffered oppression. This time they did not even cry out to God.
• God intended to use Samson to deliver the people from oppression.

• Samson's parents received special instructions for how to raise him so that he would be kept pure and focused until the day of God's appointing.

We have some notions of what Samson must have been like. If you have been raised from a child on the stories of Samson's greatness, you can probably picture him in your imagination. He might look something like this:

• Rippling muscles on a tall and tanned body.
• Long, flowing dark hair that frames a handsome face.
• Smarter than most people, using riddles to keep his secrets away from inquiring minds.

For all of Samson's gifts, though, he was still vulnerable.

A legend might take us in the direction we need to explore. An old fellow had been in the north woods for weeks by himself, camping out. Each night at dusk he built a campfire, boiled water for coffee, and took out his skillet to fry up some bacon for dinner. As he was sitting by the fire one night, the water boiling and the bacon sizzling, he heard a tremendous racket in the brush. The sound was like a roaring freight train, and as trees fell over and branches snapped, the biggest bear he'd ever seen lumbered into the clearing. On the bear's back was a tough-looking man holding a seven-foot live rattlesnake in his hands.

The big man shouted and screamed as he brought the bear to a skidding halt, bit the head off the rattlesnake, and flung it into the brush. Then he slid off the bear's back. The camper was speechless as this wild-eyed renegade walked over to the fire, tossed the boiling coffee down his throat, drank the hot grease from the skillet, and ate all the bacon in one bite.

As he wiped his hands with poison ivy and slapped the bear awake from a nap, he turned to the camper and said, "Partner, I'm sorry I can't stay around and visit with you a while, but I've got to keep moving 'cause a real bad dude is chasing me!"

Samson was one bad dude. Maybe we can imagine him riding a bear and handling a rattler. But there was a bad dude chasing him as well!

We could assume that the baddest dudes of all might have been the bullying Philistines. This neighboring group held a power over Israel that no one can quite explain. I think their power says more about condition of the people of God than about the might and sheer numbers of the Philistines.

As a nation, we are given the picture here in Judges that once again, these children of God have yielded to their passions, acquiesced to their obsessions, and partied until they can stand no more. The Philistines had developed basic blacksmithing skills and some early iron weaponry. So oppressed was the larger Israelite nation that they seemed to depend on the Philistines for these basic goods and services. And the Philistines forbade them from developing their own.

The Israelites were in such a weak position that they simply complied. Then along came Samson. The Philistines saw the threat he posed, and they began a campaign to capture and control him. He was their main target.

Once Samson was grown, he could smite Philistines by the dozens according to the stories. He could outsmart them, too. Unfortunately for him, there was an even badder dude.

Read Judges 16:4-31.
We could say that Delilah was the bad dude chasing Samson. One of his few weaknesses was beautiful women. Delilah lured him in. She even conspired to get his secrets from him. He toyed with her, using his riddles and mysteries for a while.

Delilah proved to be one of the rare people who could get around Samson's intellect. She used her charm to guilt him and her soulfulness to manipulate him. Delilah eventually melted through Samson's defenses. She would prove to be central to bringing down this mighty and powerful warrior leader.

But no. Even Delilah wasn't the baddest one chasing after Samson. Believe it or not, the one person stronger than Samson was *Samson.*

He couldn't control himself. He couldn't contain his sinful lusts or his anger and bitterness. As you read his story, you'll notice that many of Samson's feats of strength were motivated by bitterness, anger, and revenge!

I reconnected recently with an old school friend. The other day, I found myself praying to God in thanks for the life of this old friend. You see, we almost lost him. Many times, I have told my wife, Elizabeth, about this friend. In high school, I used to say that as far as common sense—"horse smarts"—he had to be the most intelligent person in our class. He is a gifted guy.

But as a teenager this friend discovered drinking and drugs. I don't mean he simply liked to party. No, this friend would go on binges he could not control. Until a few years ago, he cycled through marriage and jobs, unable to live stably. In a relapse not far back, he went into a coma at the age of forty-six. For eighteen days, my friend lay comatose in a hospital. Doctors were guiding his family to make some end-of-life decisions for him.

Against the odds, he survived. He says now that he reconnected with his will to live while he was in that coma. Upon waking up, he realized his need for God. Now he serves as a mentor and program director in a church-based support ministry. He is finally using his gifts! He is Henri Nouwen's classic "wounded healer." At the time of this writing, he and I are working to help a mutual friend overcome her chemical dependency. I have never been prouder of a person than I am of him!

We are made smart and strong for a purpose, and it's not for any reason other than to serve our Creator within the kingdom. God, who is the source of our gifts and abilities, is also the source of our direction. Apart from God's greatest hopes and priorities, our use of these gifts and abilities will miss the mark every time.

We may appear to win some victories in the short run. We all know someone—maybe it's us—who seems to enjoy every earthly pleasure that comes his or her way and still does nothing but succeed. But we also know that this kind of life rarely lasts.

This week, the headlines broke of yet another athlete who had managed to lose millions and end up broke. Another ongoing story tells of a young man who had the world at his feet and has now been kicked off his team and forfeited his scholarship. And yet another celebrity marriage has ended in the face of excess.

These were all people whom you and I might think of as somehow stronger, prettier, or more gifted than we are. But they too are broken.

Apart from God, eventually—like Samson—we can't even keep out of our own way.

God raised Samson up to make a difference in the lives of a beaten-up, pushed-about people. In the end, he came back to God and reached out for God's grace. Only then were the purposes for which Samson had been given his extraordinary gifts accomplished.

By the way, our images of Samson might not hold up against reality. After all, what was Delilah's burning question of him? She wanted to know, "What is the secret of your strength?" You would only ask a question like that after you had looked at someone and seen something rather ordinary. This Adonis whom we view as so unlike us might have been more like us than we realize. Samson is a biblical figure whose gifts may have been more supernatural than they were Superman.

And, like us, Samson was not impervious to his own weaknesses. Instead, he was capable of being brought down by a foe no farther afield than himself. Samson calls upon God's grace and finally gives himself over to God in the end. In one mighty act, Samson's strength is revisited on him as he collapses the arena where the enemy has him on display. They are in some sense defeated by this act. A greatly diminished Samson has one more moment of strength.

The Importance of Acting Now

What does your faith story look like? Are you serving God's purposes on purpose? Are you voluntarily putting the gifts God has given you to use in the tasks you were made for?

God wants to bless you. Be faithful to the call. Keep the vow you made to Jesus the Nazarene in baptism. Honor his word by following his will. Go about doing the things that matter to God. Look at all the time Samson wasted when he could have been delivering those in such profound need. Don't be like him. Don't wait. Act now. You and I are not guaranteed to have the final chance Samson had.

1. What do you wish you knew more about when it comes to Samson and his story?

_____

_____

_____

_____

2. When you picture Samson, what do you see? Why do you think he was like this?

_____

_____

_____

_____

3. Who do you think were Samson's enemies? Discuss this question with your group, and list as many as you can.

_____

_____

_____

_____

_____

4. People wondered about the secret to Samson's strength. What strengths do you believe God has given you?

_____

_____

_____

_____

_____

5. To what purpose has God bestowed these gifts in you?

_____

_____

_____

_____

_____

6. How do you reconcile the odd ending to Samson's story as he emerges triumphant over the enemy in God's last act of grace to him?

_____

_____

_____

_____

_____

7. The cautionary issue with second chances is that we are never guaranteed to get one. They are always surprises of grace. How do you believe this truth applies to your life?

_____

_____

_____

_____

8. What place do you believe the Samson story holds within God's guidance of Israel?

_____

_____

_____

_____

_____

A Disturbing End

Session 10 covers five chapters in Judges—an ambitious undertaking. As you read through chapters 17–21, you'll likely find it difficult. If people complain that some of the Old Testament is bloody and violent, then certainly this is ground zero of that complaint. Still, they too are part of our sacred literature. There is value for us, even in the pain and horror.

In his commentary on Judges, scholar J. Clinton McCann groups these chapters as one unit under the title "Complete Deterioration and Terror" (117). Doesn't that motivate you to read them?

Gideon's and Samson's legacies are brought up for us again in this section. These two prominent national heroes made choices that led Israel more toward self-guidance than into God's greatest hopes. Samson strayed from his Nazirite vow and paid a mortal price with his strength and his freedom. Gideon opened the worship system to include idols, thereby influencing the people to step further from the one God of Israel.

Chapters 19–20 contain one of the most disturbing stories yet found in Judges. We might ask *Why?* Why would our loving Creator seemingly preside (or allow) this level of violence and destruction? Another equally pressing question might be what we, the readers, are supposed to gain from this text.

Vignettes from Real Life

She has little or no job most days. What money she manages to make goes toward her out-of-control lifestyle and the occasional jaunt up north or overseas. The pictures she posts to social media make it look like she is living a great life: younger men who are fun at parties; beautiful scenery in exotic locales; fun-looking friends who appear glad to have her with them. But underneath it all is a confused, grieving, and lost person. Her midlife crisis culminated first in an affair and later in her own kids asking her to leave the home. She is broken, but she self-anesthetizes with her "fun."

He sits at the bar in the corner, nursing a drink and smoking too much. The restaurant has become his home and family. He is a well-known "regular." If you come in on a weekend, he is there. But if you stop by on a weekday at lunch, he may also be there. So ubiquitous is his presence that at times you swear he never leaves. A rumor gets spread that long ago there was quite a different chapter in his life. He was a high-achieving young executive, they say. You don't really know, though. That seems like too much of a leap for the man you see now.

Such is the story of ancient Israel in Judges. Israel had many natural resources and blessings from God, but the people proved unable to stay in close relationship with God. They brought hardship upon themselves and failed to live up to their own covenant relationship with the Creator. One can listen to Judges, or to the accusations leveled by the Old Testament prophets, and barely recognize the promising young nation as Joshua delivered to the Promised Land.

It has been suggested that chapters 17–21 reflect a predictable outcome for the era depicted in Judges. Why do we cover such a large chunk of the book in this last session?

Read Judges 17:1-13 for an opener to the action.
As we move through the chapters, we read about the following events:

1. In chapters 17–18, Micah, an Emphraimite, steals money from his mother. He eventually returns the money to her, but she gives it back under the pretext of dedicting it to the Lord. Micah uses it to hire a Levite (a man of the priestly tribe) who dreams of one day serving God as a priest. Micah gives the aspiring priest a house, a salary, and a clothing allowance and then declares himself a bona fide tribal leader. The problem is the people of Dan have no such provision. Although a large tribe by population, they were the last tribe to receive their territory allotment. The small space they were given was constantly being raided by the neighboring Philistines. This pushed the people of Dan into a nomadic existence, and kept them from setting up tribal leadership or a stable lifestyle. Eventually, they chose conquest as their solution. Even neighboring tribes within the Hebrew nation were in danger. Thus, the action we see in Judges 17–18. Eventually,

they came into Ephraim where Micah had established a place of power and stole everything—priest and all. The story ends with Micah pursuing them, only to be turned back when they threaten his life.

2. In chapters 19–20, a Levite goes on a trip through the land around the Hill Country of Ephraim. He takes a concubine from Bethlehem and settles in. After a few months, she gets mad with him and goes home to her father. The young Levite follows her. His father-in-law welcomes him, and they go on a multi-day drinking binge together. One day's revelry leads to the next. Finally, the Levite departs and takes his concubine with him. Presumably, her father's extended hospitality of the Levite has given time to heal the rift and she decides to return to Ephraim with him. On their journey home, they consider a stop in Jerusalem to spend the night. But they decide to pass on through to Gibeah in the land of Benjamin. When they are taken in to rest there, a rowdy group of men invades and takes the concubine and a servant. They rape them and kill them. A vengeful battle ensues on behalf of the young Levite. Israel squares off with warriors from ten tribes against Benjamin. A terrible war takes place, but eventually Israel defeats Benjamin at the end of chapter 20.

3. In chapter 21, the gathered representatives (or "Elders") of the tribes of Israel have compassion on the Benjamin tribe. On the one hand, because of the atrocities detailed in the previous two chapters, they swear an oath that they will give none of their young daughters as wives to the young men of Benjamin. On the other hand, they recognize that they will soon wipe out one of the twelve tribes if they deprive them of wives. So the elders devise an ambush: Hundreds of young women will be sent out to dance in a field. The young men of Benjamin are to lie in wait and pick out a young woman to kidnap— or carry off to their ancestral home and marry. This is what they do. Thus, Benjamin is repopulated and able to be sustained.

These are all strange and deeply troubling stories.

Themes in the Last Five Chapters of Judges

Though we often don't realize it, much of our life is lived in patterns. While not all of our patterns are bad, some cause unnecessary trouble.

Israel had fallen into patterns of behavior, and toward the end of the book of Judges the consequences of these patterns became even more severe. Instability and conflict were the hallmarks of this era. Conquest seemed to be the way of the land. Israel was vulnerable to invasion from every side.

Here some themes we could notice over these last five chapters:

• A slow but complete "deterioration" of spiritual Israel has been taking place during the entire book of Judges. Despite each rescue and delivery from punishment by God—and despite prolonged periods of peace under the judges—the overall curve of society is downward.

• Some believe these last chapters especially are an epilogue that in part sets up a fairer view of the Davidic Kingdom that eventually came.

• There is an emphasis on what humans want, and when they pursue those wants that are contrary to God's ways, their lives run further away from fellowship with God. In these stories, God is willing to allow the freedom of these pursuits. But, God is also willing to allow the consequences of those actions. God's ways are intended to give life. Apart from God, our actions often bring about hurt to others and ultimately to ourselves. God's greatest hopes included peace, health, and goodwill. Conquest, theft, injustice, and the like always brought about pain and death. At least seven times in these five chapters, we read something akin to the closing verse of Judges: "In those days there was no king in Israel; every man did what was right in his own eyes" (21:25). This summary observation is neither approval nor an endorsement.

• Specific issues include lack of loyalty to the one God in favor of the many (idolatry), insertion of "self" as the primary god, and unbridled pursuit of passions. The likely result of such an atmosphere is chaos, anarchy, competition, and violence—all situations we encounter in Judges.

Lessons for Us

Is the age described in Judges so different from the one in which we live now? As you read about it, what sounds familiar?

Though it may seem pessimistic, I can find several connections between the notions of a postmodern culture and the observations in Judges 17–21. There is no general consensus among scholars on the precise definition, but postmodernism is largely a reaction to the assumed certainty of scientific or objective efforts to explain reality. In essence, postmodernism is based on these positions:

• Reality is nebulous at best. In fact, reality is not reflected in our understanding of it; we construct reality as we try to understand our own individual realms.

• We resist explanations that claim to be valid for all groups, cultures, traditions, or races. The spotlight is instead on the relative truths each person gathers along the way.

• Interpretation is everything. Interpretations of what the world means to us personally yield insight.

• We rely on personal experiences over sweeping, abstract principles. The outcome of one's own experience will necessarily be fallible and relative rather than certain and universal. However, validity is granted by the individual.

• We are convinced that many, if not all, apparent truths are only social derivations. They are therefore subject to change. There is no absolute truth. The way people perceive the world is vulnerable to the roles of language, power relations, and motivations in the formation of ideas and beliefs.

We notice in Judges that Israel had no central leader and no central structure or practice. There was no uniform worship or observation of the people's heritage. They were living, in some ways, a lifestyle that might be understood by viewing it through postmodernism. There were no binding rituals, and the standard became "all the people did what was right in their own eyes." Again, we hear this repeated in 21:25 as though the writer of Judges wants us to capture this indictment and burn it into our hearts.

These final five chapters of Judges serve a cautionary purpose to civilizations. They remind us of the value of a faithful people remaining close to God. God's ways, in contrast to Israel's practice of freedom, give meaning and sustainability to life. These chapters also emphasize the need for a new way of living.

Although God was able and willing to serve as ruler or "king" to Israel, the people cried out for a divinely appointed leader just as their powerful neighbors had. In a new era immediately following the time of the judges, God would give them what they asked for. Israel's era of kings was on its way. In some ways, that too should be a cautionary tale. But of course, that is a subject for another book and another study.

1. Even within our freedoms under God, why does God allow a certain level of evil even to be a possibility?

_____

_____

_____

_____

_____

2. In the mystery of God's providence, where is God in the kind of action described in Judges?

_____

_____

_____

_____

_____

3. How does the way the people of Israel attempted to live relate to our current cultural mood of personalized ethical and moral standards?

_____

_____

_____

_____

_____

4. How fair does it seem to place so much responsibility for a people's faithfulness, or failure, at the feet of leaders such as Gideon and Samson?

_____

_____

_____

_____

_____

5. On balance, how does God's faithfulness to the people of Israel shine through?

_____

_____

_____

_____

_____

6. What does Judges have to do with us? What am I supposed to learn from this biblical book that makes my faith and my living better?

_____

_____

_____

_____

_____

7. Is there an area of your life where you think you know more than God? If so, what is it and why do you feel that way?

_____

_____

_____

_____

_____

8. What are the dangers in assuming you know better than God, and how can you change your attitude?

_____

_____

_____

_____

_____

Bibliography

Bright, John. *A History of Israel.* Louisville KY: Westminster/John Knox Press, 2000.

Callaway, Joseph A. *Faces of the Old Testament.* Macon GA: Smyth & Helwys Publishing, 1995.

Flanders, Henry J., Robert W. Crapps, and David A. Smith. *People of the Covenant.* New York: The Ronald Press Company, 1973.

Harbour, Brian L. "A Needed Deliverer," *Connections Commentary,* Connections series. NextSunday Resources, Smyth & Helwys Publishing, forthcoming, 19 November 2017.

Herzog, Chaim, and Mordechai Gichon. *Battles of the Bible.* London: Greenhill Books, 1997.

Hogaboam, Rick. "Through Literary Eyes: Judges 3:12-30: 'Ehud, the Deceptive Lefty; Sword-Induced Dung, and Lifeless Idols.'" totascriptura.com/through-literary-eyes-judges-312-30-"ehud-the-deceptive-lefty-sword-induced-dung-and-lifeless-idols"/ (accessed 4 May 2017).

Kent, Dan G. Joshua, Judges, Ruth. Volume 4 of Layman's Bible Book Commentary. Baptist Sunday School Board, 1980.

McCann, J. Clinton. *Judges.* Interpretation: A Bible Commentary for Teaching and Preaching. Louisville: John Knox Press, 2002.

Myers, Jacob M. *Judges.* Volume 2 of The Interpreter's Bible Commentary. Nashville: Abingdon, 1981.

————, and Phillips P. Elliott. Volume 2 of The Interpreter's Bible Commentary. Nashville: Abingdon, 1981.

Prosser, Bo, and Charles Qualls. *Lessons from the Cloth: 501 One Minute Motivators for Leaders.* Macon GA: Smyth & Helwys Publishing, 1999.

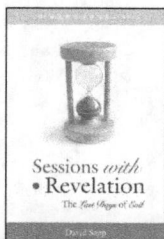

www.ingramcontent.com/pod-product-compliance
Lightning Source LLC
LaVergne TN
LVHW051702080426

835511LV00017B/2677